Street Talk

Not Angry But Hurting

A model for therapy developed
through work with women in street
prostitution 2005–2018

Pip Hockton

First published in 2019 by
Free Association Books

Copyright © 2019 Pip Hockton

A CIP Catalogue of this book is available from
the British Library

ISBN: 978-1-91138-324-6

Typeset by
Typo•glyphix
www.typoglyphix.co.uk

Cover design by
Candescent

Printed and bound in England

Table of contents

Acknowledgements

This report has been funded by Lynn and Simon Dodds, who also funded the partnership between Street Talk and the Chrysalis Project hostel for women in street-based prostitution. We learned how to engage therapeutically with vulnerable women as a result of that opportunity and have now worked closely with the Chrysalis Project for ten years. Most of our learning has arisen from the work which Lynn and Simon Dodds have made possible. All of us at Street Talk thank Lynn and Simon for their loyalty, generosity and encouragement, as well as the London Community Foundation who have given Street Talk enormous support. Together you have helped some of the most vulnerable, excluded women in our city.

Foreword

If you have opened the page, read on. This will not be easy, not least as the authors have vividly captured the stories of the women they have worked with in therapy. Reading it, even at a very long arm's length distance, as I am, is an emotional roller coaster. I found myself experiencing a storm of outrage, fury about the systemic failure of services to reach out to these women, anger about society's uninformed prejudices, touched by the courage of the women while admiring their resourcefulness and deeply saddened that people can become so de-humanised that they perpetrate terrible crimes against women.

The voices of the women come across vividly as the therapeutic approach pioneered by the authors is told through their stories. This is a population who are excluded from society and from mainstream services, who are regarded by many as less than human, who nevertheless have experienced trauma, severely disrupted lives, violence and repeated humiliation.

The therapists are all highly trained and have discovered ways of engaging with these women by applying principles of object relations theory. A central guiding principle is to help the women encounter their own humanity, to make human contact, to listen and hear their stories. This is not an easy task: we hear of the barriers to engagement and how they can be overcome by patience, compassion, courage and faith that listening, hearing and bearing witness can help release deep wounds. Turning away would be a much easier path to tread and I admire the therapists who keep the women in mind, through a journey which can involve long periods of interruption, silence and tolerance of uncertainty as the women move in and out of the therapy, living on the fringes of society.

The therapy is difficult, for the therapists and also for the women, yet despite the challenges they face the women shine through, impressing the therapists with their grasp on survival, however tenuous it may be at times, with their strengths, intelligence and resilience. They employ defences, as do we all, which include ways of escaping from emotional pain and gradually, through a sustained and consistent relationship, they begin to open up, reconnect with buried memories and sometimes find ways to join mainstream society.

The authors describe particular characteristics of the therapy, a non-punitive approach is taken, relapses happen, the setting is not conventional and therapy can take place in bail hostels or, in one case, a garden, where Grace liked to sit, the therapist finding a seat in the form of an upturned crate, having first amused Grace navigating their path through the nettles. This is a therapy of presence, of inclusion, no woman being turned away.

The clinical model is well articulated, with four stages identified, beginning with a therapeutic alliance, passive creative work, turning point and then working from a more peaceful place. Each of these stages is described, each having particular challenges. It is not often that therapeutic work taking place during a phase of non-engagement is described, as here in the passive creative stage, when the therapist continues to be mindful of the women even in absence.

Alongside the clinical model we are reminded of the many wider societal issues which result in silence about street prostitution, in effect colluding with the perpetrators of this practice and of the impact on vulnerable women.

I am privileged to have the honour of writing a foreword, to have been asked to listen as Pippa, who founded this project, initially struggled to articulate the approach she has developed with the help of her co-workers over the past twelve years. This is no surprise, paralleling as it does the experiences of the women she works with in putting the unspeakable into words. I have born witness to Pippa's journey, her training in therapy, the setting up of Street Talk through to the writing up of the work. I was witness to a period of passive creativity in which I was waiting to hear from her, receiving messages from time to time that she was thinking and writing, while also managing the other pressures of the work. Then the fully formed account of this work arrived.

It is simultaneously painful, shameful and inspiring; it speaks for itself and will form a legacy from which this work can continue to grow and develop. Sarah describes the importance of the work when she as a person is dismissed, though is not alone as she turns to her therapist saying 'You are the only one who can see.'

I thank all the contributors, therapists and women alike. I encourage you to look, read, listen and learn: if I am not mistaken this is an early stage in a wider societal dialogue that is well overdue.

Jan Birtle

Jan Birtle is a Consultant Medical Psychotherapist providing therapeutic help for people who have been traumatised and excluded from mainstream society. The challenges of this work are in reaching people who do not 'fit in' across many agencies, who have experienced adverse contact with authorities and consequently do not have societal safety nets. Jan has pioneered applications of psychodynamic therapy which allow the therapist to work side by side with the client in a collaborative manner. Alongside her clinical and training work in the NHS, Jan is an Honorary Senior Lecturer at the University of Worcester. Recognising also the importance of prevention of societal trauma, Jan sits on the Board of Trustees of Unseen, a charity working towards a world without slavery.

Introduction

Before founding Street Talk in 2005, I was practising as a therapist in the NHS, where I had become troubled by the inequalities within the provision of mental health care. It seemed that most of the patients referred for NHS psychotherapy were those who could have afforded to pay for it themselves, their referral frequently a result of their own highly developed advocacy skills. The most vulnerable patients, with more complex needs, few of whom were in a position to pay for therapy, seemed, for the most part, to be excluded.

Going further back to my training, at the Lincoln Institute of Psychotherapy, it seemed that therapy was exclusive in the real meaning of that word. As students in the early 1980s we were taught that people with a transient lifestyle, poor verbal skills or who speak English as a foreign language, those with even the most minor developmental difficulty, those using substances or alcohol or on certain prescribed medications, those with poor mental health, even those over a certain age, were not suitable for psychotherapy.

Women in street based prostitution find themselves excluded from care; they are not necessarily registered with a GP, the portal to most health services. Women are refused access to A and E on occasions, even when they are injured or critically ill, let alone access to specialist services such as psychotherapy. Street Talk was founded in a spirit of experimentation, to discover whether it were possible to engage extremely vulnerable women in therapy. It started humbly, at a drop-in centre, the Maze Marigold, in Hackney where we began to learn from the women whether, or how, they wanted to engage in therapy.

Looking back over the last thirteen years, it is possible to identify a distinct pattern of engagement. It may seem that this has been a long time coming. There is a lot to learn about the lives of women in street prostitution; after thirteen years of this work, I am still learning each day. The purpose of writing this is to define the clinical model which has emerged in order to support our own practice within Street Talk, to ensure that those of us carrying out the work, as well as those who might carry it forward in the future, have a clear understanding of the model. Perhaps there are others working in the sector who may also find this outline of the clinical practice which has emerged helpful. This is not an academic paper; it's a working manual. Honouring the fact that everything we have learned has come from the women, where possible their words have been used. Their identities have been protected.

Sarah

One day, a commotion broke out in one of the day centres where Street Talk provides a service. One of the women and a member of staff were shouting at one another, just as I stepped into the counselling room. Sarah, waiting there for her counselling session, said quietly, "When people shout like that, they're not angry, they're hurting. That woman shouting, she's in pain." Her words spoke a truth which underlies the work of Street Talk.

The Background to the Work

Late Fragment

"And did you get what
you wanted from this life, even so?
I did.
And what did you want?
To call myself beloved, to feel
myself
beloved on the earth."

Raymond Carver

Sally

The first woman who came to Street Talk at the Maze Marigold didn't know her real name. She regularly changed her name over the time that she worked with me. She had run away from care at about the age of fifteen because she was frightened of one of

*the other children. She was never brought back –
who knows whether there was any effort to find her
– and she was soon in the grip of a drug dealer who
pushed her into prostitution, paying her in crack.
By the time she came to Street Talk she had been in
that life for about twenty years. She had been run
over by a car whilst "doing a road"* (standing on
the pavement waiting for passing custom) *and had
come out of hospital with pins in both legs. It hurt
her to stand on the road at night so she had taken
punters* (customers) *back to the hostel where she
was living. This had led to her being evicted so she
was sleeping in a shop doorway. She had chronic ill
health, ulcers, tuberculosis, HIV, Hep C and was in
constant pain in her legs, on top of which she was
pregnant. She wasn't registered with a GP; the TB
was untreated; she didn't have pain killers, relying
on crack for pain relief. She was mixed race, knew
nothing of her birth family and could only surmise
her ethnicity. She didn't know her own date of birth,
age, legal name or national insurance number.
When she ran away from care, she lost that most
basic of information which most of us take entirely
for granted, but which is necessary to function
in society. She had some level of developmental
difficulty which made it hard for her to process*

information. One day she turned up to one of her counselling sessions with some of her front teeth missing. When I asked what had happened, she said that her "boyfriend" had insisted that she have sex with one particular punter. She hadn't wanted to, because that punter had hurt her before, but her boyfriend had promised to take her to Disneyland if she had sex with him one more time. She had agreed because she wanted to go to Disneyland, although she was frightened. The punter hurt her again: this time he knocked her teeth out. Sally had not believed the doctor who had told her she had HIV and Hepatitis C when she had been in hospital, after being run over, but she believed the "boyfriend" who had promised to take her to Disneyland.

Sally was childlike; she was probably in her late thirties, but presented like a girl of about ten, which may have come from a degree of fixation from childhood trauma, or developmental difficulty, or both, but her childlike understanding of the world made her catastrophically vulnerable. She didn't seem old enough to cross the road by herself, let alone to be standing working the road at night. I have put the word boyfriend in inverted commas to draw attention to the nature of the relationship which was essentially one of exploitation, where she would be working for him as well as having sex with him. Sally would describe it as a relationship based on love, perhaps because that was all she knew of love, or perhaps because it was the only kind of intimacy available to her. The word boyfriend is a loose term with many meanings in this context.

Sally showed us that there are people living a third world existence on the streets of London. Like Sally, all the women who come to Street Talk are in acute pain. They have all lived through trauma and self-medicate for the symptoms with whatever is available, alcohol or substances, which leads them into addiction. Prostitution is a desperate means to support the addiction. It brings more brutality, more pain, more trauma, and that's the trap the women are in. The chain of catastrophic events which led to Sally sleeping in a shop doorway in Dalston had begun in childhood. Her family had failed to keep her safe and equally the state had failed to keep her safe. I don't know what pain she had lived through in her early years because she couldn't remember, but at the age of fifteen she had been frightened and her child-like solution was to run away. She didn't get the help she needed at the appropriate time and that is the story of all the *women we work with. Would a child who had been in a car accident be left to cope with their injuries, to cope with the pain without help or treatment at the right time? The only difference is that Sally's injuries in childhood weren't visible.*

How is it possible that Sally was living in a doorway, not accessing benefits, not housed and not getting health care? Why are there women living this third world existence in twenty-first century Britain, a country which, to many, is defined by its National Health Service and welfare system? There is not one answer. Women end up destitute, relying on drug dealers to put a roof over their heads, in a crack house, or rough sleeping as a result of a complexity of factors which contribute to their vulnerability. It is necessary to have some sense of some of the barriers which prevent women on the street from accessing care, in order to understand why Street Talk has responded to that unmet need in the way that it has.

Societal Denial

Children are prevented from telling anyone that they are being abused. There is a systemic failure of services to recognise and respond to abuse, vulnerability and trauma in childhood and adolescence. The instinctive response of a victim of sexual abuse is one of shame, which leads them to conceal it, to feel that they have somehow invited the abuse upon themselves, that they are culpable and complicit.

Almost all the women who have come to Street Talk have grown up in the state care system, where they have lived transient lifestyles, shifting from one foster carer to the next, moving from one part of the country to another, frequently missing out on a secondary education in the process. The transient way of life prevents children or adolescents from forming lasting relationships with carers or teachers, which is compounded by the retention problem within social work, which results in constant changes in social workers for children, preventing close, consistent long-term work, precluding any kind of relationship from developing. A child who is experiencing abuse is rarely able to tell a stranger.

Those women who have not grown up in care have grown up in very troubled families where most experienced multiple forms of abuse.

Laura

Laura grew up in a family where she and her three sisters watched their father gradually beat their mother to death. Their father was never brought to justice for his violence. Their mother never brought charges and no agencies brought charges on her behalf, even following her death from domestic violence. Laura was sexually abused by her father and beaten horrifically throughout her childhood and early teenage years until she left to live with a boyfriend when she was fifteen. The family were known to social services. Laura had periods with different foster carers but had many periods when she and her sisters were returned to the care of the father. She missed out on most of her education as a result of the movement in and out of care and when she was in the care of social services, between foster carers, most of whom were out of borough, some as far as Cornwall and Scotland. She described the happiest time of her life as a time when she was in foster care with "an old lady" who lived by herself in a house which "was full of old-fashioned stuff which smelled old". The best thing about that time was that she had a teacher who remembered her name. She loved school and her greatest regret is that she missed out on her secondary education. She said that she likes to stand near to schools to watch the children come out at the end of the day "... with all their stuff, sports kits, musical instruments, books, lunch boxes. I wish I could have had a bag with all that stuff and been piling out of school, struggling to carry it all, with my friends. That must be the happiest you can be. I can't think of anything more beautiful to look at than that. It cheers me up to watch them."

Laura came to Street Talk at a hostel for women in prostitution; she was chaotically using drugs, including large quantities of crack, supporting the habit through prostitution. She had given birth to four children, all of whom had been removed. She had not had any contact with family members for seven years and had served multiple short prison sentences. She described her happiest times in recent years as the times when she was in prison because she was never lonely there. When she was in prison she had a job, leading the team of cleaners on her wing, and took a lot of pride in making sure that all the cleaners got a coffee and a biscuit. In therapy she disclosed that her greatest fear was that her children would learn that she had been sexually abused by their grandfather; she said she would not be able to bear the shame of them knowing that about her; anything was preferable to that. She was in her thirties when she came to Street Talk and had never before spoken about her experiences of abuse in childhood. During the period that she was working with the Street Talk therapist, she ran into her father in the street in South London. She hadn't seen him for about fifteen years. They chatted for a few minutes, he told her he had just come out of hospital, then, as she said goodbye and turned to leave, he swung a punch which sent her sprawling into the road and broke her two front teeth.

The therapist got a chilling sense of how vulnerable Laura had been as a child, in the care of a father capable of such unpredictable violence. Like almost all the women who come to Street Talk, Laura turned to crack to relieve the pain of the symptoms of trauma from what she had lived through in childhood. She is a highly intelligent woman who would be the first to tell you that crack didn't solve anything, but it was her only resource to provide temporary respite from symptoms which in her case included suicidal feelings, agoraphobia and depression. Like for most of our women, crack was what enabled her to get through the day.

Laura's case shows how children are prevented from feeling safe enough to tell someone what is happening. In spite of many periods in the care of social services, when her mother was incapacitated through domestic violence and after her death, no professionals knew that Laura and her sisters were being beaten and sexually abused throughout their childhood. Laura and her three sisters had no choice but to cope with that by themselves. Women learn to keep their story to themselves in childhood because professionals don't create the relationships which are conducive to trust. There is no arena where experiences which children experience as shameful can be reported. The silence imposed in childhood becomes habitual and the experience of self-blame and the sense that the abuse is deserved repeats itself throughout life.

Kate

Kate had grown up in a large family where life revolved around the church community and which, from the outside, might have given the appearance of being a caring family. However, from when she was about eleven, her father raped her each Sunday, when the family got home from church, making her mother and her brothers watch whilst he did it. As she got older her father used to rape her, then make her brothers rape her too, while the rest of the family were made to watch. That was her family life. She grew up believing that was normal. When she came to Street Talk she was about fifty, hovering between crack houses and rough sleeping, involved in prostitution and chaotically using substances. She had made many attempts on her own life over the years and, like a lot of the women Street Talk works with, was taking her own life slowly through extreme self-neglect.

Kate committed an offence during the period that she was working with Street Talk for which potentially she may have been given a custodial sentence. Kate is a gentle, intelligent, timid woman who had never previously been in the criminal justice system and she was very afraid. Having been referred by the Judge to the probation service, she was reluctant to attend the appointment and found it very difficult even to be in the waiting area. The interview room frightened her because there was no window and she suffered from claustrophobia. She approached the meeting, which was her opportunity to explain the circumstances of the alleged offence, as something to get over as fast as possible. Also, like many of the women, she wanted to "say the right answers". The probation officer had a tick-box questionnaire, of which one of the first questions was, "Did you have a happy childhood?" Kate replied "Yes", because she thought that was the right answer and she wanted the interview to be over. The probation officer naturally moved on to other questions and Kate's opportunity to explain something of her life story, which might have been taken into account when it came to sentencing, was lost. I had been allowed to attend the interview with Kate and I was able to interrupt the interview. I asked Kate to tell the probation officer one thing about her childhood. Kate thought for a moment and then said, "I jumped off the roof of our house when I was fifteen because I was pregnant and I didn't know whether the baby's dad was my dad or one of my brothers and I didn't know what I would tell the baby."

The outcome on that day was that the probation officer recommended a non-custodial sentence. However, the point of this episode was that it illustrates how challenging it is for women who have experienced childhood trauma to advocate for themselves and this is in part how they fall through the net of social care.

Kate had no other family who were able to advocate for her and she was not able to do that for herself, so when she was charged with a serious offence she inculpated herself by her failure to offer an explanation for what had happened. Kate was silenced in childhood. It is hard to break that silence.

Almost all those women Street Talk has worked with who have been given a custodial sentence were charged for offences which arose when they were trying to defend themselves from men who had dominated, frightened and abused them, in some cases for years. One woman who had been kept locked in a cupboard for two days by a man eventually broke down the door, accidentally cutting her captor in the face with a piece of splintered wood as he tried to hold her in. She was not able to say anything in her own defence, too frightened of how her abuser would punish her if she dared to report him. She did not tell the arresting officers or the duty solicitor that she had been locked in a cupboard for two days without food or drink. She was charged, convicted and given a custodial sentence for actual bodily harm. By the time I visited her in prison she was in solitary confinement on the segregation wing, where prisoners are punished for infringements of regulations: the prison within a prison. She had not come to the attention of the prison medical services, but it was evident that she had slipped into a psychotic breakdown which was almost certainly why she had got into trouble in prison and been punished. It was a harrowing visit to someone whose treatment at the hands of the criminal justice system ironically and agonisingly replicated the terrifying ordeal which had landed her in prison.

Being Disbelieved

The 1,400 cases of child sexual abuse which took place in Rotherham evidenced how hard it is for children who are experiencing exploitation to get help. Women who have experienced similar abuse to those who grew up in Rotherham come to Street Talk from all over the land. It's not a Rotherham problem, nor is it confined to cities: women come to Street Talk who have been abused in tiny villages, small towns and big cities. It is not confined to any particular ethnicity: abuse is universal.

Perhaps the greatest lesson from the retrospective scrutiny over that one particular period, 1997 to 2013, in one town was that many of the children abused had tried to report it but were not believed by the police or social services, with the exception of youth worker, Jayne Senior. Those women who had the courage to speak out and ask for help in childhood report that they were either blamed for the abuse or accused of lying. That experience repeats itself throughout their lives.

Jane

I accompanied Jane to a child protection case conference earlier this year. It was an important meeting for Jane who desperately wanted to be able to evidence her parenting capacity and to keep her two children in her care. As we took our seats in a room with about fifteen professionals, some of whom were previously known to Jane whilst others were strangers, the social worker said, "Before we start I would just like to say that Jane tells a lot of lies, so be careful what you believe." The social worker had met Jane twice before the meeting.

Having worked with Jane over six years, I knew her to be an open, honest woman, who reports events accurately and clearly. She had overcome obstacles which seemed insurmountable to get herself off the street, to exit prostitution and to provide a home for her family. Later in that meeting the same social worker reported that Jane was unwilling to engage with professionals and was hostile. Whether the social worker was conscious of her provocative behaviour or not, she demeaned Jane, who had come to the conference with goodwill and optimism that morning, but was left feeling both powerless and angry. Could anyone blame her for not engaging with professionals?

Women do not Choose Street Prostitution

There is an assumption amongst some service providers that women have chosen this lifestyle. This may come in part from the complexity of the term prostitution. There may be a conflation between the indoor prostitutes (*women working in organised brothels, massage parlours or from their own home*), who have a platform based on their right to choose prostitution, and women working on the street, for whom prostitution is not a choice. Street Talk has not worked with one woman who has chosen street prostitution. It is violent, dangerous and humiliating. It is not a choice when someone can only support themselves through selling their body; that's desperation, it's the choice of a cornered animal.

One might make the case that what the different groups have in common is that they all sell sex. It is not even that straightforward. Much of the activity street prostitutes are involved in is violent, a playing out of power and oppression. Street Talk is currently working with a woman who has a punter who pays her three pounds a time to defecate into her mouth. Is it appropriate to call that prostitution? It is not selling sex. It is someone paying to abuse a vulnerable person who has no choice and who is so used to abuse they can't identify it any more.

Semantics may contribute to the failure in services for women who are trapped in street prostitution. Whilst there is only one word to describe so many diverse activities and, whilst so many misconceptions surround the concept, how can there be a clear understanding of the causes of street prostitution and of the psychological issues for those involved? The semantic limitations, the lack of a word to describe the activity of one person paying another to defecate in their mouth or to describe the activity of a person having sex with a woman who is forced either by others or by circumstances to do that, must account in part for the failure of services. There is no language.

Since founding Street Talk I have been constantly frustrated by the widely held assumption that women are in street prostitution from choice. To attribute street prostitution to a woman's choice is to collude with the abuse which has brought her to that place. That assumption is rarely made about trafficked women who are more widely perceived as victims. There is broadly more compassion towards trafficked women and most donors are more willing to support services for trafficked women on the basis that they "are not there from choice". It is true that trafficked women have not chosen prostitution, they have been forced, deceived and brutalised, but the same is true of the women working the street.

Professionals Unconsciously Punish Women

Women who are abused and neglected in childhood become trapped in a catastrophic chain of events, where they find themselves making desperate choices for which they are punished over and over again throughout life. They are frequently perceived as culpable by professionals who consciously or unconsciously punish vulnerability in women in a number of ways. Women learn to believe that they deserve to be punished, which works to emphasise the unconscious self-loathing which accompanies childhood abuse. The expectation that they will be held responsible for their own vulnerability and punished prevents women from engaging with professionals. It is very common for women to find it almost impossible to attend appointments with court, the probation service, social services, lawyers, benefits agencies and addiction services amongst others. When women miss these essential appointments it can lead them into a vicious downward spiral. For example, when a woman becomes pregnant she is afraid to hear that the baby will be removed, afraid to be told that she is not fit to be a mother, which frequently makes her reluctant to have a pregnancy test and to engage with ante-natal services. At a later stage her late engagement with ante-natal services will be cited as evidence that she did not care about the baby and lacks parenting capacity.

Martha

Martha owed a drug dealer twenty pounds and when she was not able to repay the money he punished her by raping her with a sword. She survived because it happened near enough to the hostel for her to be able to crawl back there, where staff immediately called an ambulance. Her punishment did not end there. She went to theatre where she was operated on for nine hours. The next day she was told by hospital staff that she had asked for this. She was discharged, without pain relief, without anti-biotics, with no provision for aftercare, with nothing but an instruction not to have sex. She was not signposted to addiction services, psychiatric help or social services. The police were not involved, in spite of the brutality of the attack. Martha was never going to dare to bring charges against the drug dealer; look how he punished her for defaulting on a debt of twenty pounds. The message to her from the professionals involved was that her life has no value.

This case also draws attention to the vicarious trauma experienced by front line workers. The hostel staff on duty on the day Martha was attacked were traumatised by what they saw. The manager, who had previously been an A and E nurse, said she had never seen anything which distressed her as much. The staff were equally distressed when Martha turned up at the hostel the next day having travelled on the bus, in pain, hours after being on the operating table. The neglect women suffer goes further than instances of neglect arising from a failure in compassion or understanding from individual professionals or teams, such as the medical team who treated Martha. There is a systemic failure to provide care for women with complex needs.

Ethos of Personal Responsibility

There was an outpouring of public revulsion at the brutal abuse of Peter Connelly in 2007. He was a baby, so he wasn't held responsible for what became of him, but how much public interest is there in his siblings who also lived through abuse and have had the usual disrupted journey through the state care system? At what point does sympathy fall away for a person who has that kind of start in life and at what point do they begin to be held accountable for their suffering? The women Street Talk works with have lived through some version of the start in life which Peter Connelly had and, although they have survived, they have suffered, as he suffered, but, at some point along the way, they find themselves held responsible for their suffering and blamed for behaviours which are driven by trauma.

Unbearable Reality

This work has taught those of us working for Street Talk the meaning of the word unspeakable. There are things that have happened, and which still happen, to women, which are hard to speak about and which can't be written about here. It takes women years to tell some of what they have lived through and when you hear it you can't repeat it. This leads one to question whether one of the reasons professionals disbelieve women and deny their truth is that this represents an unconscious defence from an unbearable reality. It may be that to deny the reality of the women denies one's own vulnerability. If a woman has become extremely vulnerable through no fault of her own, then, by extension, that can happen to anybody, which makes the world precarious and unsafe. If it should be the case that to acknowledge that the brutality the women have lived through is unbearable, is unconsciously pushed away, then how can professionals provide for their needs? There seems to be a vicious circle where denial of the reality of the women's experiences prevents services from responding to their needs, keeping women trapped in a lifelong cycle of abuse and trauma.

Failure in Mental Health Services

The women who come to Street Talk are catastrophically failed by mental health services. It seems virtually impossible for women with acute mental health needs to access the care they need. Women with complex mental health issues which do not fit easily recognisable diagnoses seem most vulnerable to neglect. The diagnosis of personality disorder seems to be used as a blanket diagnosis, with little evidence of any treatment being made available. It seems to be used as a label for patients who exhibit challenging behaviour, closing down any further investigation or professional responsibility. None of the women who have had a diagnosis of personality disorder seem to have had a thorough discussion of the meaning of their diagnosis with professionals. Many only discover that they have been diagnosed with a personality disorder when their medical records are investigated as part of family proceedings. It is a diagnosis which serves to dismiss them from mental health services, leaving them with little understanding of their own mental health or hope of any improvement in the frequently disabling symptoms which brought about the diagnosis. I would go as far as saying that the words "personality disorder" are less a diagnosis than a life sentence.

Women are refused access to mental health care, even when they are in danger of self-harming or of taking their own life. Looking back over thirteen years of case histories, not one of the women Street Talk therapists have tried to have admitted to hospital when they have been psychotic, or at acute risk of over-dosing, taking their own life, of putting themselves in extreme danger, have been admitted to hospital. Without exception, after presenting at A and E at times of extreme vulnerability, they have been sent back out onto the street. This is the outcome even when the woman has been accompanied and even, on one occasion, when the Street Talk therapist spoke to the consultant psychiatrist for an hour over the phone before the woman presented to A and E, when the psychiatrist gave an assurance to the therapist that the woman would be admitted. In that case, in spite of the full co-operation and goodwill of the consultant, the woman, who was accompanied by her Street Talk therapist, still failed to get past the gatekeepers at A and E who refused to make the phone call to the psychiatrist who had been prepared to have her admitted.

The most significant failing in mental health care for the women Street Talk works with is an acute failure in the provision of care for people with dual diagnosis (*who have both a mental illness and an addiction*). Approximately seventy per cent of the street-working women who come to Street Talk are dual diagnosis. Of those women none of them has ever been treated simultaneously for their addiction and their mental health issue. All of them have been turned away, sometimes repeatedly, from mental health services on the basis that their mental health symptoms are driven by the addiction. They were mostly signposted to addiction services, but were too mentally unwell to have the capacity to engage with addiction services, with the result that they were left with no treatment. They were left on the street with neither mental health care or help with their addiction, with catastrophic consequences, including custodial sentences or death.

Rachel

Rachel arrived at the hostel having served several years in prison where she had become abstinent. Most of the women in the hostel were chaotic users and involved in prostitution. Rachel was desperate to be moved; she had left prison with hopes of a fresh start, which seemed impossible in this place where she was surrounded by crack. "This is the worst place for me. Please help me to get out of here," she begged, explaining that she had been plunged back into the world which had got her into the criminal justice system in the first place. It was not the fault of the hostel staff; she had been failed by the prison resettlement services. It was utterly inappropriate to accommodate her in that hostel; presumably, it was her history in prostitution which had led to her being accommodated there. In spite of the progress she had made in prison and her determination to have a fresh start, she had not been permitted to leave behind the label of prostitute.

One week later she came to see the counsellor but was already addicted. Her mental health deteriorated catastrophically over the following months. She refused her kidney dialysis and the nurse who runs a weekly clinic at the hostel estimated that she would only live for about three weeks if she continued to refuse treatment. At that point Rachel had acute depression with frequent suicidal urges which she had acted upon many times, usually overdosing. She had been discovered unconscious by hostel staff three times following overdoses, each time taken to hospital by ambulance. The overdoses were attributed to her substance use and she was never referred to psychiatric services and each time was discharged within hours. The last time I saw her in the hostel, the whole side of her face was black with bruising where she had hit her face on a radiator when she collapsed. She said she understood that she would not live if she refused dialysis, but that was the only way she could be sure she would die.

The usual course of action working with someone who is so acutely depressed that they are a danger to themselves would be to refer them to psychiatric services, with a view to their being admitted. Once again Street Talk tried, without success, to have

Rachel admitted to hospital. The only course of action available which could save Rachel was to report her for breach of bail, to have her recalled to prison where she would be forced to have dialysis. Rachel was arrested and taken back to prison. Street Talk continued to work with her weekly in prison. The first week she was so angry with me that she couldn't bring herself to speak to me. The second week she was looking out for me before I arrived, eager to start the session. She opened with, "I know why I am here. I know how all this started." She went on to tell me what had happened to her at the age of five. She had been dragged away from her friends when they were playing in a park, tied up, raped and left hidden under bushes. Unlike most of our women she had a family, but they had no idea how to help a five year old through such an experience: what family would? From then onwards, she was afraid to play with other children and life spiralled down. She was eventually excluded from school and slid into the youth criminal justice system. Until that day in prison, Rachel, who was in her forties by then, had never spoken about that event all those years earlier. She continued to work with Street Talk, made progress and her depression became less acute, at least no longer life-threatening. She was held in prison for about a year when she was released to a bail hostel, to serve the outstanding term of her sentence.

It was brutal having Rachel recalled to prison, but she had been catastrophically failed by mental health services all her life. She had not had the appropriate help in childhood following her trauma, and in adulthood had not been diagnosed or treated for depression, in spite of repeated and serious attempts on her own life. From childhood onwards she was punished and eventually labelled as a criminal for behaviour which was driven by her lifelong attempt to manage her trauma. It was heart-breaking that when she was acutely depressed she was safer in prison than in the care of mental health services.

Grace

Grace became psychotic whilst she was living in the hostel for women in prostitution, suffering from persecutory hallucinations, talking with the figments of her hallucinations, crawling naked on the floor in the hostel, urinating in public and at times becoming aggressive. The hostel staff and

Street Talk therapist did everything possible to get her a mental health assessment, diagnosis and treatment. However, because she had an alcohol dependency she was consistently batted away from mental health services on the grounds that her psychosis was alcohol induced, and signposted towards addiction services. It was evident that her alcohol dependency was driven by undiagnosed psychotic illness, her way of self-medicating for the tormenting symptoms. She was far too unwell to have the capacity to attend an appointment with addiction services.

On days when she was well enough, Grace liked to sit in the shed in the garden of the hostel. It is a dump, long neglected, surrounded by weeds and brambles, but that was where she felt safe and she found it funny to watch the Street Talk therapist clamber over the nettles and sit down next to her on an upturned crate. The aim of the work was just to make some human contact, to get to know her. The therapist got glimpses of a brilliant, creative woman who loved her children more than anything, who wrote songs, who thought and cared about lots of things. She had a great sense of humour and liked to lament how the "... world has been bungalised". When she was well she did some creative work with the Street Talk art therapist which inspired us all. Her dream was the one most of our women hold: a place of her own, her children back, an ordinary life.

One day last year, passers-by found Grace unconscious in the street, not far from the hostel, and called an ambulance. When she came round she struggled to get away because she had a terror of hospitals and it seems that in her struggle she bent the thumb of one of the ambulance crew. She was charged with assault, but didn't turn up to court, probably because she was too unwell on the day to know where she was supposed to be, or what day it was. A warrant went out for her arrest and she was sentenced to several weeks in prison. In prison she had no contact with psychiatric services. Following her release from prison, Grace moved from one hostel to another, always evicted after a week or two as a result of behaviours driven by her psychosis. It was an assault on a member of the public which eventually precipitated her admission to a psychiatric ward, three years after the Street Talk therapist had first requested it. She was diagnosed as bi-polar, prescribed, and within six weeks she was stable, functioning and abstinent. Since she left hospital she has started writing and recording music, lives independently and now has regular contact with her children.

Her case demonstrates that her addiction was driven by her mental illness. When she finally got the mental health care she needed, she quickly became well. Grace has four children with whom she has contact although they are in the care of their father. It was not only Grace who suffered from the neglect of her mental health; the children who were not able to have contact with their mother whilst she was mentally ill suffered too. One might go as far as suggesting that signposting dual diagnosis patients to addiction services whilst denying the underlying mental illness which is driving the addiction is iatrogenic.

The Challenge of Anomalous, Complex Cases

Many of the women who have come to Street Talk over the last twelve years have had extremely complex mental health histories, with multiple enmeshed issues. They are not cases which necessarily fit comfortably with common diagnoses and it feels as though enough is not known or understood to provide them with the care they need. This points to a broader issue of the lack of research into mental illness. Is it that women with complex needs are too complex for providers of mental health care?

Fitting Out Rather Than Fitting In

There are many examples amongst the Street Talk client group where women have highly individual behaviours which are harmless, but which become pathologised by professionals and used against women, simply because they don't conform to a norm. It is a question which has relevance for all of us practising as therapists: does therapy coerce clients towards societal norms? How much room within the practice is there for self-expression?

> *"People may well make sense of their own experiences in a different way to professionals."*
> (Kalathil, 2011)

Cathy

Cathy is a transgender woman of Middle Eastern ethnicity, who had at some point had some surgery to transition from man to woman, privately in

Bangkok. The treatment was incomplete and had left her in constant pain and, whilst she clearly and consistently identified as a woman, the incomplete surgery had left her physically in a kind of gender limbo. She was pathologically attention-seeking, exhibiting many extreme behaviours, for example standing in the middle of the street to try to stop traffic, shouting out to strangers in the street, sometimes provocatively, sometimes making random accusations. One of her behaviours was to travel on public transport with a goldfish in a bowl, telling other passengers, bus drivers and passers-by that she had been bullied by the goldfish. She was addicted to substances and worked to support her habit with both male and female punters, getting beaten up on the street at least once a week. She had several stays in one of the hostels where Street Talk provides a service, but these always ended in eviction following fights with other residents who found her disturbing. She was desperately lonely and isolated, but her constant provocative behaviour prevented her from forming friendships. It is extremely difficult for transgender women who evidently don't want to use men's services, but who frequently encounter hostility from the other women in women's services. It is not unusual for transgender women to be ostracised and bullied by women in women's services. This was Cathy's experience in the hostel.

Cathy had a fantasy family with a wife and two sons and this was mostly what she talked about in her therapy sessions. She went into great detail about the lives of the fantasy wife and sons, recounting family arguments, homework grades, football practice, favourite meals and school trips. She frequently showed the therapist photographs of the family which she had cut out of magazines or newspapers and which were always different. The fantasy was enduring and seemed to be in some way sustaining, providing a narrative which ran alongside the reality of her own life, almost like a television soap. Touchingly this fantasy was an expression of what most of the women who come to Street Talk want, a partner and a family of their own, some version of a so-called normal life. The mundanity of the fantasy family life was in sharp contrast to her own life which lurched between arrests, clubbing, chaotic substance use, sex working, beatings and fights in the street. She lived with a broken jaw from being beaten up in the street which had never been properly treated and one wondered how much her substance use served as pain relief as well as relief from childhood trauma.

Cathy did succeed in accessing a psychiatric assessment with a psychiatrist who was sympathetic and who did his best to engage with her. However, at a joint consultation between the psychiatrist and the Street Talk therapist, he said, "Cathy, there's no medication for attention seeking." He was honest and what he was saying was that he had no idea what to do with this woman who put herself at risk daily, through her extreme behaviours. The psychiatrist did his best but Cathy defied diagnosis. Her case illustrates the limits of psychiatry, even when mental health professionals are compassionate.

Cathy made many choices each day which flouted norms. Some of her choices put her at risk, but alongside the risk-taking behaviours were many harmless behaviours such as writing all over her body, from head to toe with eye liner which she did meticulously each day. Why shouldn't she do that? That was part of her highly thought-out look, which bordered on performance art. Her extreme appearance, which took her hours to bring about each day, not only sustained her, but it may have been an unconscious act of defiance. In spite of physical and mental pain, poverty, illness and loneliness, her body was a work of art each day. Her appearance was the one thing she had control over and in its own way it was a liberating act of self-expression and courage, an assertion of self against the odds, a garden in the desert. In her utterly idiosyncratic way, Cathy was magnificent. Does therapy encourage self-expression, choice, creativity, or is it reductionist? Does therapy reduce people to narrow norms of self-expression? It is worth examining how the therapist might unconsciously influence a client who has chosen to push norms of behaviour and self-expression; it is possible that in such cases therapy may peddle norms which are unwanted by the client and that therapy itself becomes an oppression. Cathy was challenging, but at least some of the challenge came from her creativity through her sexual identity, her appearance, her fantasy life, none of which were anti-social; in fact they were pro-social, just different, out of the ordinary.

Removal of Children, Unseen Grief and the Escalation of Trauma

The removal of children and the unseen grief which that brings is an overwhelming issue in the lives of many of the women who come to Street Talk. There have been women, as in the case of Peta given below, who have had their baby removed in the days following the birth but who, with the right support, would have parenting capacity.

For many of the women who become caught up in street prostitution and all which that brings, their story began with their removal from their birth mother, moving from one foster carer to the next, missing out on the love of a family, never forming stable attachments and missing out on education which is disrupted with constant moves. Women facing the removal of their child are in agony, fearing that their baby will go through the state care system and will live the life of abuse and trauma which they have known. Others had their children removed long before coming to Street Talk, intensely guilty, racked with self-loathing, and many feeling they have failed their own child. One of the women Street Talk worked with had previously had six children removed when she became mentally ill. That woman wrote six letters a day, one to each child and kept them in boxes, hoping to give them to each child if they came back to find her in adulthood, so they would know how much their mother loved them. She was living out of her car, which was stuffed to the ceiling with the boxes of letters. She was afraid of going to a hostel in case she was prevented from keeping the letters.

Family proceedings are punishing and draconian; child protection case conferences consist of the mother, frequently alone with nobody to support her, round a table with numerous professionals, most of whom she will not have met before, including the police, social services and health services. There are usually large rolls of paper hung from the wall, upon which the Chair invites the professionals present to write their concerns for the child. It is not infrequent for the walls to be covered with negative statements about the woman. The mother's entire history, as it is known to services, is brought up, often in a judgemental tone, with conjecture, hearsay and assumptions always slipping into the mix. It is an inhumane process. Over the years Street Talk has supported many women through case conferences, all of whom have left feeling demeaned, judged and worthless. It is not unusual for women to find it unbearable and to run from the room crying. At the next meeting the baby's social worker will almost certainly write up on the wall charts something along the lines of, "Mother left the previous case conference before the end. Hostile and not sufficiently interested in the outcome for her baby to remain for the entire meeting."

Not all the women working with Street Talk who have aspired to keep their baby have succeeded in making enough progress, or are well enough, to be able to take care of their child. In these cases, the role of the Street Talk therapist has been to support the women through the grief of the separation. Street Talk works with such a small number of women: there are many women who have their children removed who have no support with the grief, increasing their vulnerability to self-medicating with whatever is available, getting deeper into the deadly cycle of prostitution, exploitation and violence. One of the ways in which women comfort themselves after the removal of a baby is through another pregnancy, even though they know that that baby will be removed too. For that nine months of pregnancy they have someone to love. The poor care for vulnerable women with complex needs who become pregnant creates more vulnerability and in some cases a second generation of vulnerability. Sometimes the process of child protection proceedings compounds a woman's sense of worthlessness. When it is necessary to remove a child from the care of a mother, it must be possible to do that with compassion, humanity, to acknowledge the woman's trauma and to offer an appropriate intervention. I was present with a woman when social services came to the hostel where she lived to remove her child. Two social workers arrived, with police, who rattled handcuffs at her, shouted at her to stand on the other side of the room, refused her permission to kiss the child goodbye and refused to accept the little teddy bear which she had knitted for the baby and wanted him to have. At the most vulnerable moment of her life, she was treated like a criminal. There is currently a vicious cycle, where suffering engenders further suffering. A woman who is so vulnerable that she has her child removed is unlikely to have the resources to recover from that experience on her own; few women would. It is the responsibility of providers of mental health care to address that need. It is not a need which is currently met.

Underestimated Strengths, Intelligence and Resilience

These women have strengths which tend to be underestimated or not to be seen by professionals. It takes immeasurable courage to face another day when you are tormented by the symptoms of trauma. It takes resourcefulness and intelligence to survive on the streets. The women have the capacity to be infinitely tolerant and compassionate to people who are suffering and have a heightened awareness of the suffering of others.

Whilst there are the inevitable conflicts between women which characterise all human relations and which do spill over into violence at times, there is an underlying community on the streets where most women find some companionship and friendship, frequently fuelled by humour. Whilst their behaviour may be judged by professionals as anti-social, their community evidences that much of their behaviour is pro-social.

Many of the women have the ability to take great pleasure in small things. Recently a woman was waiting to meet the Street Talk counsellor outside Camberwell Court. When the counsellor arrived, the woman was sitting on a bench looking up. "The sky is so beautiful today. I just want to sit and look at it," she said. What a gift. All the women have their talents and insights which are unique and precious. It may be the overwhelming complexity of their situation, or it may be the transitory nature of the relationship which prevents professionals from discovering the individual strengths and attributes of the women. Whatever the reason, when professionals see only the pathology and the anti-social behaviours they are missing the whole and, in so doing, alienate their client.

> *"Stigmatising language, denying people's full potential... are examples of getting in the way of recovery and desistance."*
> (Deegan, 1988; Harris and McElrath, 2012)

Imposition of Inappropriate Solutions

One of the consequences of professionals failing to discover, to appreciate, the individuality of each client, failing to understand their personal world, is that the wrong solution to a problem can be imposed which sets the client up to fail.

Ruth

Ruth was evicted from her home whilst she was pregnant and forced to sofa-surf. She had lived on and off the streets for ten years and was well established within her community of women in similar circumstances. She was very sociable and took great pleasure from the companionship of her friends as well as making good use of the services for vulnerable women on her patch of north London. The support staff from one of those services helped Ruth to get independent accommodation shortly before the baby was due. With the best intentions, they chose a room in a house in south London on the border of Kent, on the basis that, of the accommodation available, that room was the biggest one, in the best area, an area with parks and coffee bars, possibly an area which seemed attractive to them. Ruth wanted to stay on her own patch, but the decision was made for her and reluctantly she moved in with catastrophic results. She gave birth shortly after moving, in a hospital which was entirely unfamiliar to her, where she was too far away for friends to visit. She left hospital with the baby, to a room where she lived in utter isolation in a neighbourhood far from anyone she knew, removed from her community. Her isolation in that vulnerable post-natal period contributed to her depression which ultimately resulted in her having the baby removed.

Pia

Pia had been rough-sleeping but eventually got off the street and into a hostel. Shortly after she moved, a rough-sleeping woman asked her to mind her dog for a few minutes, but never came back, leaving Pia with the dog. She kept the dog, smuggling it in and out of her room in the hostel where pets were not allowed. The Street Talk counsellor tried to persuade her to get rid of the dog, fearing that she would be evicted and back on the street when it was discovered by the hostel management. Pia took no notice and it turned out that the responsibility of taking care of the dog provided her with a daily routine and the motivation to reduce her substance use. Over the next six months, she engaged with an addiction service and exercising the dog regularly seemed to lead to her eating better and generally taking much better care of herself because she knew the dog was depending on her. Pia eventually made sufficient progress that the hostel management referred her for a flat of her own.

In this case it was the Street Talk counsellor who tried to impose an inappropriate solution.

Simplistic Societal Solutions

Sometimes there is no solution to a woman's problem. The challenge in those cases is to recognise that and not to try to invent a solution because it is too painful to acknowledge that there isn't one. There is a societal myth that if you work hard, roughly behave yourself, observe the law and exhibit good citizenship, you will be okay. There is an expectation that if the homeless get off the street, get a roof over their head, get off benefits and into work, start paying their own rent and contribute fiscally, their own problems will be solved and they will cease to be a problem to the public. It is not that simple.

Laura

Laura's background was referred to above. She was one of the most vulnerable women who had presented to Street Talk, in a life of chaotic addiction, multiple accidental overdoses, repeat offending, homelessness, the removal of babies and involvement at the most exploitative end of street prostitution, regular beatings and injuries. She arrived for her counselling session one day during this period complaining that she had been flung off a bus for smoking crack upstairs. Over the following years, she gradually emerged from that place, motivated when her fifth baby was removed. She said to the Street Talk counsellor, "My life can't get any worse. I want to fix up, so when Gabriel grows up and comes to find me, he finds someone worth finding." The counsellor agreed to give all the help she could. When she came back to the hostel the following week Laura was waiting for her and said, "I have changed my mind." The counsellor's heart sank, fearing that she had lost hope of recovery, but Laura went on, "I don't want to wait for him to grow up to come to find me. I am fixing up now and fighting to get him back." Over the next three years, Laura did all that was asked of her. She became abstinent, sustained detox and rehab, exited prostitution, underwent parenting assessment, attended parenting classes, as well as therapy with Street Talk, and took part in an enterprise training provided by an organisation called HERA and finally avoided contact with the list of people she was not allowed to meet with. The result of her determination was that she was awarded full parental responsibility in the family court for her fifth child, got a home of her own, took some courses and got a job. She also got back in contact with her other children who had been removed in the past and was building relationships with them.

She fulfilled the societal expectation of recovery in all respects. However, on minimum wage, as the sole provider for two people living in London, she could not quite make ends meet financially. At the end of each month, she fell slightly short, perhaps as little as twenty pounds, of meeting her utility bills. Over a year or so this accumulated and, without family to turn to, she faced the option of taking out a loan, a short term solution with dire long term financial consequences, or returning to prostitution. She chose prostitution after six years off the street, intending to work just a few nights to make up the shortfall in her household expenses, to pay her arrears and get the household budget back on track. On her first night she was beaten up by a punter which triggered the memories of the violence she had experienced in childhood and, within a week, she was back on crack, self-medicating for trauma. Over the following months she had her son removed and lost the family home.

Nobody could have tried harder to get well, to realise the dream the women share of living an ordinary life, of providing a loving home for her child, than Laura did. She jumped through all the hoops: detox, rehab, supervision orders, case conferences, court appearances. She studied, she found the best work she was able to. She said the best day of her life was the first day she went to work, "I just wanted to show my boy that you get up and go to work. That way he won't grow up to be a gangster. That's all I ask from this life." It was not enough.

The Case for a Specialist Therapeutic Service

The barriers to care for the women are as many and as complex as their own tangled life stories. The most effective barrier is the women's anticipation of prejudice, the fear of attending any kind of appointment, which may come from their expectation that they will be humiliated by the professional. There are practical problems: a transient lifestyle, chaos, poverty, not having the bus fare, violence, being beaten up and just the physical inability to get themselves somewhere. Some of the women have never heard the words counselling or therapy and have no idea what that would involve or how it might help them. Why would somebody go to see a counsellor when that means nothing? There is a combination of psychological, emotional and practical issues which knit together, to make it virtually impossible for women in street prostitution to get even the most basic help. The failure to access care combines catastrophically with the pathology of trauma to keep them trapped in a devastating cycle of abuse and trauma, leading to vulnerability and more abuse.

The Aim

The aim of the work with the women is to enable the women to encounter their own humanity in the relationship with the therapist. We aspire to what are referred to as soft outcomes: women feeling worth something, feeling human, getting some sense of their own identity. The so-called hard outcomes – exiting prostitution, abstinence, getting out of exploitative relationships, getting children back from the state care system, moving into independent living, getting onto benefits or into work or education – are important, but it seems that when the soft outcomes fall into place the hard outcomes follow. However, the value of the work is in the human contact, irrespective of the outcomes which may ensue. One woman told us after some years that her turning point came when the Street Talk therapist passed her in the street, noticed that her shoe laces were undone and bent down to tie them for her because she had mobility difficulties and couldn't reach. She said afterwards that in that moment she felt human again.

"People must be able to imagine themselves beyond the identities of addict, offender, or mental health patient. This new identity must also be reaffirmed by others."

(Farrall, 2005)

Not all the women who come to Street Talk make the kind of progress which can be easily quantified. Relapse is part of the process for most women but the encounter with one's own humanity, which lies at the heart of this work, takes place even for those women who are not in a position to improve their lives at that time. Looking back over the twelve years, some of the work which has been most worthwhile has been with those women who died, some of whom had been struggling with illness, whilst others have died suddenly and unexpectedly. Either way, it has felt very privileged work, to create some kind of human contact at the very end of a woman's life. Such work does not fulfil any kind of outcome measures but is nevertheless important and worthwhile. It is impossible to describe how moving it is to work with a woman who has suffered all her life, to accompany her in her last months or weeks.

Inclusion

In the introduction, I referred to the exclusive nature of psychotherapy, as it was taught in the 1980s. The case for excluding some people is that they are not robust enough, for one reason or another, and that therapy might de-stabilise them, causing more harm than good. Whilst one understands that argument, it presents a crude, binary division between those who are fit and those who are unfit for therapy. Over the last thirteen years Street Talk has engaged with hundreds of women, all of whom might have been excluded according to the training I had. All those women have taken some small benefit. For a few, that small benefit has grown and for others that small benefit may yet grow into bigger benefits. We have learned two important lessons from working with people with mental illness and addictions. The first is that there are therapists skilled enough to work with people who are not mentally robust without de-stabilising them, without triggering a relapse. It is possible to enable a vulnerable woman to encounter her own humanity without raising her anxiety. The second lesson is that there are people who are in grave danger, who would not have long to live without help, and in those cases to refuse to engage with them might be more harmful. Therapy might be their best chance at survival.

Clara

Clara was working in an indoor brothel, but shared the background of most of the street working women: abuse, growing up in care, followed by sexual exploitation in her late teens after leaving care. She had survived multiple overdoses and had finally got a funded place in detox. The consultant told the Street Talk therapist that he had never encountered a patient with so many different substances in their body simultaneously and in such quantities. He was fearful that she would not survive detox. He asked whether the therapist thought he should go ahead with the treatment. The reply was, "She won't survive if you don't."

Clara survived detox, went on to rehab with Nelson and has now been abstinent for six years. There is a parallel with women who are left to cope with trauma without help. There is some risk that therapy might be disturbing and potentially might make women more vulnerable, but if they don't get help there is a much greater risk that their lifestyle will kill them. That is the reason why Street Talk is as inclusive as possible and, so far, has never turned a woman away.

Theoretical Basis, Qualifications and Experience

The work is rooted in object relations theory, which provides a theory of relationships between people, with particular emphasis on relationships within the family. The basic tenet is that we all strive to find loving relationships and that relationships experienced in one's early years will influence one's ability to form relationships in adult life. The therapists are trained in object relations theory and all are qualified to Master's degree level and have years of experience of working with people with complex needs. The work is challenging and practitioners need that confidence in practice which comes with experience.

Supervision

One cannot overstress the importance of finding supervisors who are not only well qualified and experienced, but who also have experience of working with people who have a history of trauma and who are currently experiencing extreme disadvantage and complex needs. In addition, supervisors need to understand why the work differs from conventional practice and to have the confidence to adapt to a variant model. Therapists mostly start out taking on just one client for Street Talk, building up to a maximum of six, and supervision is weekly, allowing supervisors to offer close support.

Alongside the individual supervision, there is monthly group supervision where therapists can discuss cases and both learn from and support one another.

Practical Adaptations to the Therapy to Overcome Barriers to Access

The practical adaptations to the clinical model have not influenced the therapeutic work which adheres to the same boundaries, principles and professional code of conduct, as therapy practised in other contexts. The adaptations to the service are as follows:

Outreach

The therapists work in the hostels and day centres for women in street based prostitution and for women who have fled from traffickers. Many of the women do not have the capacity to travel or to attend appointments and, for many, mistrust of professionals and dread of being disbelieved or judged impedes their attendance of appointments. It helps the women to work in a familiar non-medical setting. It creates that home ground feel.

Partnership model

Most women who come to Street Talk are clients of the day centres or hostel which means that there is shared responsibility for the welfare of the women. It would be impossible to work in isolation with women who have such acute needs. The partner organisations have support staff who are able to respond immediately to the practical issues. Those women who have made progress are those who engaged with multiple agencies, if not in the early stages, in the later stages of recovery. A significant aspect of the work is to encourage women to engage with other services and any success can never be attributed to Street Talk or to any sole organisation; it always comes from working together. Street Talk is a small cog in a big wheel.

> *"The journey becomes easier with the cumulative increase in social and personal capital, which means access to more resources and healthier ways to cope with adversity and pain, and so relapses and setbacks become less frequent."*
> (Harris et al, 2011; Farrall and Calverley, 2006)

Becoming Part of the Furniture

The therapists wait between sessions in the communal areas in the hostels and day centres. Staff at the partner charities introduce new clients to their service to the therapist, in order that the women know who the therapist is and have some understanding of their role. There is an art to being present and accessible without crossing boundaries; the therapist has to become part of the furniture: there, but almost forgotten until required. The purpose is to raise the women's awareness of the therapeutic service available, whilst minimising their anxiety about professionals. A measured degree of familiarity is essential to the inclusivity of the service. Knowing the therapist, if only by sight, seems to be one of the factors which enable women to make an initial approach to the service at a time of crisis.

No Waiting List

The women who come to Street Talk at the hostels and day centres are seen on that day with no waiting. It takes courage to ask to speak to someone and, given that women first come when they are in crisis, it wouldn't work to offer them an appointment at some future date. Women in the hostels know which day the therapist will be there and know that they can always spend some time with them on that day.

Length of sessions

Length of sessions are adapted to women's needs. Some women want to start with short sessions of perhaps twenty minutes. For others just to take a few minutes to get the feel of the therapist is enough. Very few begin with a fifty minute session but usually women become able to sustain that length of session as they get used to the process and learn the importance of boundaries. Sessions do not exceed fifty minutes.

No penalty for non-attendance

Women are not punished in any way for non-attendance. They are always welcome back after any length of absence, whether or not they give a reason. In the later stages when women get used to attending regularly they take great care to let the therapist know when they are prevented from attending. An absence might only be interpreted in terms of object relations theory, once a woman has established a regular pattern of attendance.

Continuity of care

The women live transient lifestyles moving from one hostel to another, finding themselves evicted, sofa-surfing, or rough sleeping, with many sudden changes. Continuity is provided by taking therapy to women who go into prison, hospital, rehab and bail hostels. Women who move into independent accommodation or a different hostel have the opportunity to continue the work at the Street Talk therapy room. Sometimes contact is maintained with telephone sessions when women move away from London or don't have the capacity to attend. Letters are also written to women in prison or rehab or to those who have relocated to a different part of the country.

Women who have ended their work with the service know that they would be able to come back and have support in the future should that be appropriate. Given the extreme circumstances of their background, it is much easier for them to return to the service where their history is known.

Advocacy alongside therapy

There are occasions when the therapist may be required to act as a witness in court for a woman, to attend a meeting with the probation service or to attend a child protection case conference with a woman. Naturally, this does influence the therapeutic alliance. The adaptation to the conventional boundary is carefully managed and there is no evidence that that the dual role of advocate or witness has impeded the work, even when the outcome of a case conference or court hearing has not gone in the favour of the client. It would have more influence and possibly damage the relationship were the therapist to fail to attend court or other meetings where there is the opportunity to represent and advance the interests of the client. Our experience has been that when the therapist is required to advocate for a client, therapist and client experience a shared purpose and a shared momentum which has strengthened the therapeutic alliance. It is shocking that women can appear in court where life changing decisions will be made but nothing is known of their background. The role of the Street Talk therapist is to provide at least some relevant information about a woman's history.

Sarah

Sarah, referred to above, appeared before the family court, hoping to be granted permission to keep her child. Not one of the professionals – the baby's social worker, Sarah's own social worker, the baby's guardian, the legal teams, or the judge – who were weighing this life changing decision for mother and child, knew the basic facts of Sarah's own story. Sarah had given birth to her first child at the age of eleven in the bathroom of her foster carer's home. The father of the baby was the foster parent, who killed the baby, then took his own life. Nobody in that court knew about Sarah's own trauma. When the case had been heard and the professionals had left the room, Sarah turned to the Street Talk therapist and said, "You are the only one who can see."

The only person in that room who knew something of the life Sarah had lived and how agonising this court hearing was, stirring up old trauma and grief over the baby who had been killed, was the Street Talk therapist. The professionals, making life changing decisions, did not know because they had not asked.

The importance of helping a woman in this way when the opportunity occurs needs to be examined in the context of the extremely uneven relationship of power between therapist and client. The women have so little power and much reduced, if any, agency, which places the responsibility on the therapist to take an opportunity to represent the interests of the client when that arises. Over the years, there have been many examples when women working with Street Talk have been awarded asylum in the immigration courts, been sentenced to a non-custodial sentence rather than a custodial sentence in the criminal court or been awarded parental responsibility in the family court, on the basis of a positive report from the Street Talk therapist, when there have been no other agencies in a position to provide a report. It would not be possible to work with women who have had their human rights diminished then to stand aside when there is an opportunity to influence judgement in a woman's favour. One of the injustices which disempower the women is that their history, and in particular their mental health history, is not taken into consideration by those in positions of authority.

Jane

Jane escaped from her traffickers with her one month old baby and one year old baby, the father of whom was the trafficker. After she escaped she tried to get a job as a cleaner at a hospital which led to her being charged with entering the

UK on a false passport. A family from the church Jane had joined in London had offered to babysit whilst Jane was in court. The judge in the criminal court concluded, "I do not believe your story of the trafficking and I do not believe you have children," whereupon he sentenced Jane to a year in prison. She served six months of the sentence. On release she learned that she had been refused asylum as a result of her criminal record.

At this point she came to Street Talk where she showed the therapist a letter from her trafficker, telling her that he had heard that she had been refused asylum and would be repatriated to Nigeria. The letter told her to leave the babies with social services in London, because he had arranged to have her killed when she got back to Nigeria. She shook with fear when she showed the therapist this letter. The Street Talk therapist was called as a witness at the final appeal for asylum. Jane's barrister had presented the letter from the trafficker as evidence. The barrister for the UK Border Agency accused Jane of writing the letter herself. When the Street Talk therapist was called to the stand the judge pointed out that three previous judges in criminal and immigration court had not believed Jane. She asked why she should believe the Street

Talk therapist rather than her judicial colleagues. The Street

Talk therapist replied, "because anyone can make up a story but you can't pretend to be afraid". The judge took her word and Jane was awarded asylum. A year later, the gang of traffickers, including the father of Jane's babies who had written the letter referred to in court, were caught and are now serving a prison sentence in the UK.

On that day, the intervention of the Street Talk therapist made the difference between life and death. There was no case for the therapist to refrain from appearing as a witness in order to preserve the therapeutic alliance.

Street Talk Clinical Model: An Art not a Science

Honouring the fact that the model adopted by Street Talk evolved from the use the women have made of the service over the last twelve years, it seems appropriate to begin with a case history, one which has been chosen because it is representative of those women who have worked with Street Talk over a number of years and who have made good progress.

Peta

Peta came to the Street Talk counsellor in one of the hostels for women in street based prostitution. She is of Irish background, but had been involved in street prostitution and chaotic substance use on the streets of London for seventeen years at the point when she presented to Street Talk. She was in her late thirties, well liked and respected by the other women, known for not getting involved in fights and for staying out of trouble. She presented with a relationship issue and attended a series of about four weekly sessions whilst she was troubled by her relationship. Over the following eighteen months she checked in with the therapist from time to time, usually just spending a few minutes telling her how she had been doing. Peta then asked if the therapist would see her weekly again because she had made the decision to stop using and needed help with that. She made very good use of the therapy over the following ten weeks, attending regularly and using the process to reflect thoughtfully and honestly. She understood that she needed to engage with drugs services in order to jump the hurdles to get a funded place in rehab. She made steady progress, going to a detox clinic for two weeks where the Street Talk therapist continued the weekly sessions. She was referred straight from detox to rehab in a different city where, with the permission of the management, she was allowed to continue the counselling sessions with Street Talk by phone. She did well for five months, remained abstinent, put on weight, looked much healthier and participated well with the day to day activities at the rehab. At the five month point, she and another resident *went out one night together and used crack. Peta was honest about her relapse with the rehab team, but was immediately evicted. She came back to the hostel and within a day was chaotically using and working again. The therapist made contact with Peta at the hostel, but she did not engage at all, not even in passing. The therapist let it be known that she would be available if Peta needed her. Nineteen months passed, during which time Peta did not make any direct contact with the therapist although there was some tenuous contact: news of her from staff at handovers at the hostel or from other women who mentioned her from time to time.*

One day, having not seen anything of her for nineteen months, the therapist arrived at the hostel to find Peta waiting for her. She got straight into the session, as though she had seen the therapist the previous week. She was pregnant, she wanted to keep the baby and she needed help. Peta continued to use chaotically and to work the streets throughout her pregnancy. The therapist made herself available to Peta every week of her pregnancy; she did not have the capacity to attend in any kind of regular way. The therapist would knock on her door at the hostel, but mostly Peta asked her to leave her alone. She checked in from time to time, using the sessions mostly to tell the therapist how much she wanted to keep the baby, becoming overwhelmed with grief at the thought of having the baby removed. She was caught in a common psychological trap which the women are vulnerable to during pregnancy. Peta loved the baby from the outset and it wasn't hard to understand the vicious circle she was trapped in, using crack and heroin to relieve the terror of losing the baby which then was then exacerbated by her self-loathing for using and potentially harming the baby, as well as increasing the chances that the baby would be removed. Peta found herself trapped in a self-destructive cycle.

The therapist attended the social services case conferences with Peta, to advocate for her to be given another opportunity to go through detox and rehab following the birth. The case conferences were harrowing for Peta. A Street Talk mentor, a volunteer, also supported Peta through the case conferences and on one occasion, when Peta walked out in tears, the mentor followed her and succeeded in persuading her to come back into the room.

When Peta was seven months pregnant her brother was kicked to death on the street. Peta went into premature labour at his funeral and was admitted to hospital. She had a drug dealer as her birth companion; he was the only person she had. He robbed her whilst she was in labour, taking all the cash from her bag. She used crack several times throughout her labour and at one point there was a commotion in the hospital when another drug dealer, claiming to be the father of the baby, arrived demanding to be allowed in to the secure unit where Peta was. The police were eventually called to remove him.

Peta gave birth to a baby addicted to opiates and crack, who also had syphilis. Both mother and baby were very unwell following the birth, the baby was withdrawing and they were taken together to the high dependency unit. At that point the situation for Peta and her baby was very difficult and there seemed little hope for that family staying together.

As soon as Peta was out of the high dependency unit the therapy with Street Talk resumed at the hospital. Peta had to prepare for a hearing in the family court and the therapist had to work closely with her to prepare for court. Two weeks after the baby was born, the baby was removed to be placed with a foster carer. Peta had to appear in court within an hour of her baby being removed: it was a tough day for her.

Peta had been referred by social services to the Family Drug and Alcohol Court (FDAC) who would supervise her detox and rehab process, as well as managing her contact with the baby over the next year. Ultimately the FDAC judge would decide the future for the baby. The referral to FDAC was positive for Peta: it would allow her a year, rather than the usual six months which women are permitted, to demonstrate her parenting capacity. Street Talk has worked previously with women who have gone through FDAC who have always welcomed Street Talk working alongside them, offering continuity to our client and working as a team to give the women the best chance.

Peta went back to the detox she had been in two years previously and once again the Street Talk therapist went there to continue the counselling. From there Peta went to a rehab in London where the manager gave permission for the Street Talk therapist to work weekly with Peta in the rehab. It was whilst she was in rehab that Peta was able to commit to the therapy, attending weekly, fifty minute sessions. She knew that succeeding at rehab was essential if she were to be given a chance at parenting her own child, but whilst she was there she began to place a very high value on the therapy which became an end in itself. One day she opened her session with the words, "I know why I am here." She had experienced a breakthrough where she had realised why she had started using substances in the first place as a teenager. For the first time she was able to identify the causal link between her experiences of loss and trauma in childhood and her addiction.

The next week Peta took the therapist to look at the red brick garden wall, pointing to a place where the brick had crumbled. The therapist wondered what they were looking at. Peta explained that was where she could get a foothold, climb over after dark, go and use crack, then climb back in, undetected. She said she never stopped thinking about that bit of crumbled wall.

Peta was expressing how much she had to lose and how terrifying that was, how much easier it would be to fail now, rather than risk getting what she most wanted. Is there anything more terrifying than having your dreams fulfilled? How many people have the courage to allow their dreams to become reality when the opportunity presents itself?

Peta didn't climb over the wall and sabotage her success, but steered a remarkably even course. She remained abstinent, transferring from rehab to a hostel and, by the time the baby was eighteen months old, the FDAC judge gave Peta permission to have the baby back in her care, placing her on a supervision order. It was an outstanding achievement. Frustratingly, mother and daughter had to remain separated for a further six months whilst the local borough found appropriate housing for them. Street Talk continued to work with Peta throughout this period and throughout the year of the supervision order. At the end of that year everyone was back in court again to hear the judge award Peta full parental responsibility, with no further involvement from any agencies. At Peta's request the judge insisted that the local authority provide childcare to allow Peta to continue to see the Street Talk therapist weekly for a further year.

From experience we have learned that when women make this kind of progress and finally achieve their goals, it is in fact a particularly vulnerable period. For these reasons the Street Talk therapist worked with Peta for about another year after she was awarded full parental responsibility. She continues to do very well and both she and her child are in good health. Peta has broken the cycle of abuse and the person who has benefitted most is her child who is loved, well cared for and living a good life with her own family.

Therapy of Presence

The model which has evolved over the last twelve years has always been and continues to be client led. The women who have come to Street Talk have defined the therapeutic work according to their own rhythm and at their own pace.

> *"I need to learn to walk at their pace and not mine. It can only be done at their pace."*
>
> Edwina Gately

It has taken thirteen years to write up the clinical model because it was necessary to look back over the work, to identify the patterns of engagement which have emerged. Whilst each woman's experience has been individual, it is possible to map out a distinct pattern of engagement for those women who have made significant progress. It is this pattern of engagement that has formed the basis of the four stage model which Street Talk practices.

The term "Therapy of presence" has arisen from the importance of the presence of the therapist throughout the process, including those times when the client is not present.

Accompaniment and bearing witness is central to the therapy and connects all four stages, including those periods when women are absent or attending intermittently. Sarah Anderson's paper "*The Value of 'Bearing Witness' to Desistence*" examines the importance of accompaniment in the work of Street Talk.

> *"Drawing on Object Relations Theory in work with women who had, for the most part, experienced significant trauma, 'bearing witness' – and related ideas from psychoanalytic psychotherapy such as holding, containing, and accompaniment – were presented as both an activity and outcome of the service's work... The women's accounts emphasised that one of the most beneficial aspects of the service for them was presence, in Cody's three senses; temporal and emotional 'accompaniment' on their journey, reiterated through physical accompaniment at significant life events, such as family court proceedings."*
>
> (Anderson, S. et al, 2014)

Therapy in Four Stages

Stage 1: The beginnings of the therapeutic alliance: "How can I know that I can trust you?"

Women usually ask to see the Street Talk therapist at a time of crisis, when something traumatic such as a serious attack or rape, an overdose, or other event which makes them feel particularly vulnerable has happened. It is frequently an experience which involves survival, either their own or that of someone else who is significant to them. Women typically attend about five sessions at this stage which may be anything in length between twenty to fifty minutes, according to how long they can manage. The focus of the sessions at this stage is mainly on the recent event which brought them to the therapist and their immediate relationships with hostel residents and staff.

During this phase the client tests the therapist, discovering whether the therapist is a person who can be trusted, the client feeling their way with some caution. At the same time the client is getting accustomed to the nature of the relationship and there are the tentative beginnings of a therapeutic alliance. The client will often ask questions such as, "How can I know that I can trust you?" or "How can someone like you help someone like me when you know nothing of my life?" Reasonable questions which should be asked, although not necessarily easily answered.

This phase is usually too brief for the therapist to begin to work with the transference, or to come anywhere close to making any interpretations. The therapist offers some containment which may be a woman's first experience of containment within a relationship. During this phase the therapist looks past the client's immediate trauma and their defences, the acting out, to catch a glimpse of their humanity. This forms the basis of the counter-transference which is fundamental to the next phase. Although this phase is short and the client may not manage fifty minute sessions, something significant takes place during this phase. Almost all the women come back to the therapist to do some serious, committed work at a later stage, when they are ready. This period of initial engagement seems to lay the foundations for the therapeutic alliance which will develop at a later stage. The women hold on to that experience and carry it with them, putting it to one side until needed.

Stage 2: Passive creative work: "You didn't give up on me."

This is the phase of the work which most distinguishes the Street Talk model from other models. This is a difficult phase for women as well as for the therapists.

> "... [therapy] is not an easy option. It requires demons to be confronted: many women find it harder than prison."
>
> (Corston, J, 2007)

During this phase the client more or less withdraws from the therapy, only making intermittent and informal contact with the therapist over a period which may last up to four years. The client makes occasional contacts, sometimes just a few words in passing or a message sent with another woman, that seem to serve to reassure the client that the therapist is still there and still willing to work with them. The therapeutic alliance is supported by those occasional contacts made by the client, who seems to be communicating that they have not forgotten the therapist, they have not ended this process; it is a gentle tap from time to time on the therapist's door. Occasionally the client may ask to see the therapist during this phase, but usually for an isolated one-off session.

Throughout the period the therapist continues to be available to the client. The counter-transference which began to form in the first stage sustains the therapeutic alliance through this phase. It is important to the client that the therapist remains engaged and is willing to pick up the work at any point over this period. When the client is ready to engage in a more regular way, to go on to the next phase, they look back on this period as one where the therapist has maintained their belief in their capacity to recover, and this forms the foundation of the therapeutic alliance over the next critical stages. Looking back over this period women have frequently said, "You didn't give up on me." It is evident that the experience of the therapist waiting patiently, without putting a time limit on the wait, provides a significant, positive experience for the woman. It is crucial that the therapist keeps the woman in mind throughout this period, remembering her experiences.

"They did not overwhelm us with their optimistic plans for our future but they remained hopeful despite the odds. Their love for us was like a constant invitation, calling us forth to be something more."

(Deegan, 1988, p.3)

Looking back over the last thirteen years, the women who have worked with Street Talk, with only one or two exceptions out of hundreds of women, have needed to step back from the therapy for a period. It seems that a period of latency is integral to the process which within Street Talk we have come to refer to as passive creative, the antithesis of passive aggression. There are periods in this work when the client is absent, during which the therapist holds the therapeutic space and holds the client in the countertransference. As with passive aggression, whilst there may be no activity, there is intention.

"Most journeys of recovery involve shifts in motivation, action, and circumstances."

(Farrall and Calverley, 2006)

Although the client is not engaged in the conventional way throughout this phase, there is nevertheless some small tenuous engagement, which possibly relies on no more than the memory of an earlier session, but it is this phase which eventually leads the client to the third and most creative phase of the work.

The challenge for the therapists during this second phase is to feel confident with the rhythm of the work which allows for a long period when the client is mostly absent. The women who have come to Street Talk have their own pace and their own rhythm which it is the responsibility of the therapist to adapt to without judgement and without negative interpretation. The conventions of therapy, the fifty minute sessions, evenly paced, a week apart, work well for people who have a minimum of stability in their lives, who are not living in chaos. The women who have come to Street Talk over the years have demonstrated that one can engage with a therapist in an entirely different way and ultimately achieve the same outcome.

> *"Continuous and flexible support, that is not time-limited, is important."*
>
> (Maruna, 2001)

The continuity, referred to by Maruna, in this case is created by the continuous presence of the therapist.

Stage 3: Turning point: "I know why I am here."

This is the stage when women make an active choice to engage with Street Talk. Looking back over the cases it was striking that those women who made significant progress all encountered their turning point four years after they first presented to the service. This was sometimes precipitated by a significant life event, such as a pregnancy or a bereavement which made them reflect on their own life, or sometimes it was an experience which made them fear that they wouldn't survive unless something were to change. Whilst these are the most common events which bring women back to the therapy, there is a range of circumstances. It is evident that women have to find their own motivation before they will engage with commitment.

Once they are motivated, women return to the Street Talk therapist and organise to have weekly sessions which last for the full fifty minutes, even when to do so involves travelling across London or further. Attendance during this phase is very high, the momentum picks up, the therapeutic alliance strengthens, and it is during this phase that the therapist is able to work actively with the transference. This stage lasts for eighteen months on average. In some cases women were offered the opportunity to take up counselling with a different agency at this point, perhaps as part of family proceedings, but, without exception, the women have insisted that they continue the work with Street Talk. Where the court has ordered counselling as part of a sentence or, in the case of the family court where counselling is as part of a care plan, in every case women requested that their lawyer insist that the counselling be provided by Street Talk.

Women tend to come to this phase of the therapy with a goal, which may be to get their child back from foster care, or to get well enough to make contact with family from whom they have been estranged, or to live a little longer. The goals will reflect the motivating factors and come from the women. Women frequently come back to the therapist at the start of this stage with the words, "Will you help me to....?"

Whilst women come to this phase with a specific goal, object relations therapy works closely with the client's experience of relating, the observance of the client's shifts between the depressive and the paranoid schizoid position, and the work with both the projective identification and the transference. Those women who come back to the work at this stage have the capacity and commitment to work with these concepts.

At some point in this stage women have sometimes said, dramatically, "I know why I am here", or words to that effect, at a point of insight, when they have made the connection between childhood events and their current situation. Peta said those words when she was in rehab after her baby had been born and Rachel said those words at one of her sessions which took place in prison. The women's lives are extremely complex: traumatic experiences in their day to day lives obfuscate the facts of their earlier lives and, for many, growing up moving from one foster carer to the next, they don't have the shared narrative of their lives which people who grow up in loving families have. This makes it hard to unravel events, to put the facts together in a way which creates a coherent narrative. Sally did not know her age, her name, her ethnicity or anything about her birth family, including whether she was removed from her birth mother or voluntarily given up to the state care system.

That moment when women begin to make sense of the connection between the events and relationships of childhood and those of adult life represents a therapeutic turning point, where women begin to free themselves from the deep rooted, unconscious shame which comes with sexual and other abuses in childhood. They begin to distinguish between the self and the abusive actions of others, over which they had no control and for which they had no responsibility. This third stage is a period of discovery and release for the client, an untangling of suffering. It is a rich and deeply rewarding time for both client and therapist. It is worth the wait, even when that wait lasts four years. The important thing is that women have to find their own motivation which is always unique; our work is to be there when they do.

> *"Nothing inherent in a situation makes it a turning point."*
>
> (Maruna, 2001: p.24)

Stage 4: Working from a More Peaceful Place

"I am starting out now. This is the first time I have been able to look back to understand what has happened, how I got here and to look forward to see where I want to go. I never thought about those things before. I was on the run. This is my beginning." Peta.

Across the sector there is a general understanding that recovery occurs when a woman becomes abstinent, exits prostitution, moves into independent accommodation and, in some cases, has parental responsibility for her children. When women achieve these goals, professionals tend to withdraw, not least because services are stretched and can't justify continued involvement. What we have learned from the women is they are vulnerable to relapse at this time. Having achieved goals they have strived for over years they can feel a sense of anti-climax, as well as a loss of direction which can be disorientating. The dream of an ordinary life is just that, ordinary. The drama they have become accustomed to is replaced by mundanity. Instead of appearing in court on Tuesday, women have to remember to put the bin out on Tuesday. They are frequently accommodated in an area where they feel isolated because the tendency is to accommodate women out of borough where there will be less chance of encountering people who might trigger cravings. Women frequently experience a profound sense of loss at this point. They have lost their old familiar community of drug dealers and working women and suddenly they find they have also lost their support network of professionals. For women who have lived communally all their lives, the adaptation to living alone or alone with a child is challenging. After being used to having company at all hours of the night and day, solitude is extremely difficult and this is what the women we work with struggle with the most.

Street Talk continues the therapy with women over this period, but it is at this point that there will be a contract between the client and the therapist to decide when the work will end, which may be in six months or a year, according to the circumstances of the woman. Women experience something of a shift in perspective at this point; the establishment of a stable routine, free from trauma and free from the pressure to achieve specific outcomes, enables a rich, insightful period in the therapy. Women have the freedom to consider what they want for themselves in their future without having to jump through hoops imposed by other professionals, and this is often a time when women go back to revisit deep hurts from their earlier life. It is a creative but deeply reflective period when the past and the future come together.

Recovery seems to depend on making sense of how one came to hurt all the people one ever loved and how one made self-destructive choices. When Laura, referred to above, was awarded full parental responsibility, there was an atmosphere of celebration in court, professionals were congratulating her as well as each other. The judge wept with joy. Laura ruptured this mood when she stood up and reminded the room full of jubilant professionals that she still grieved for her four other children, who had been removed and who had grown up without their mother. What she was telling us was that, whilst we professionals were celebrating, the experience was a much more complex one for her.

This period post so called recovery, is one where women can examine that complexity and make sense of their recent triumphs alongside their previous losses. Rather than measuring success by outcomes, it might better be measured by the sense that women make of their lives once they have achieved their goals. Women feel not only that deeply embedded instinctual shame experienced universally by anyone who has been sexually abused, but alongside that women feel self-loathing and a different kind of shame for the people they have hurt along the way: family, their children, the people they have loved. This is the stage when women confront grief and some of that grief is for the loss of the life they might have led and for the person they might have been if they had lived a different life. It is a period of grief, of knowing that other people, sometimes children, have also suffered. To enable the women to reconcile with the self might be our primary goal with them, and it is at this stage when that work mostly takes place.

Once the women have reached the agreed end of their work with Street Talk they know that if a crisis should happen in the future they can return to the therapy, and there have been women who have ended at the point when that felt right, but who have come back when something has happened to make them vulnerable again.

It is very common for women who have reached this stage to want to use their own experiences to help other people who might be struggling with similar issues. When women have ended their own work with Street Talk, some take up the opportunity to volunteer with us as mentors. Almost all of the women who reach this stage want to work with vulnerable women. None has expressed material goals; their goals are always altruistic.

The Work in Practice

Trafficked Women

Alongside the work with women who are involved in street prostitution, Street Talk works with women who have escaped from traffickers. It is interesting that there is considerably more public compassion and generosity towards women who have been the victim of traffickers than there is for women in street prostitution. Whilst it is not easy to raise funds for women who have been trafficked, it is considerably easier than it is to raise funds for the women on the street. There seems to be some sense that the trafficked women are more deserving, are victims, whilst the women on the street are there from choice. The background of both groups is very similar: women in both groups come from a history of extreme vulnerability. Some of the trafficked women have come from extreme poverty in third world countries or war-torn regions, but, as with the street women, most have known abuse or neglect from childhood which has made them vulnerable to exploitation. Prostitution is no more of a choice for either group. Both groups are forced into prostitution. Neither group has chosen their situation

One of the differences between the two client groups is that few trafficked women have had access to substances or alcohol. It is easier to engage with the trafficked women because their recovery is not complicated by addiction.

Street Talk works in partnership with the hostels and day centres for trafficked women, enabling women to see a therapist within days of arrival at the hostel. Most of them have made a harrowing escape from their traffickers, on top of the trauma of being trafficked, everything that they have lived through at the hands of the traffickers, and all that made them vulnerable to trafficking. Almost all the women are experiencing some level of post-traumatic stress disorder when they arrive at the hostel. There is substantial evidence to show that someone who has lived through trauma has a much better chance of recovery when there is a prompt intervention.

Women are dispersed from the hostel typically after a stay of six months. Street Talk offers ongoing therapy after they have moved away, and this may take place over the telephone when a woman is dispersed outside London. It is a frightening time for women when they move away from the safety of the hostel, when women who are already vulnerable are at risk of becoming more so. They have no family in this country and most have no friends or even contacts. They are moved away from the only people they know, frequently to nothing more than a room which they may have to share with a stranger. Some of the privately owned accommodation is overcrowded, insanitary, chaotic, Dickensian and far from any concept of a home. The shocking housing is a separate issue from the provision of care by Street Talk but it is impossible to write about the experiences of the trafficked women who come to Street Talk without commenting on that.

Women who escape from traffickers have to take on the UK Border Agency once they escape if they want to remain in the UK, applying for asylum or leave to remain. There is an assumption, as in the case of Jane, that women are illegal immigrants. Where possible the Street Talk therapist will support the woman's application to the court with written reports as well as acting as a witness when requested. So far, all those women seeking asylum, supported by Street Talk, have been awarded asylum. It cannot go without comment here that it is inhumane to ask a woman who has lived through the trauma of escaping from traffickers to take on the British legal system. Women who have been forced into prostitution feel deep shame and self-loathing and when women first escape from their captors they have sometimes been known to make up a story to cover the fact that they have been forced to sell their body. When they come to make their substantive interview as a part of their application for leave to remain, some months later when the truth of their situation has emerged, the discrepancy in their statements can be used against them in court. Street Talk is campaigning for the initial interview to be discounted in legal proceedings on the grounds that women were not mentally well enough in the hours following their escape to make a legally binding statement.

Isabel

Isabel, who was nineteen when she came to Street Talk, had left Albania with her boyfriend who took her to Italy, apparently to start a new life there and to get away from a marriage arranged by her father. The boyfriend dropped her off at a house while he went to park the car. She knocked at the door where she had been dropped off and this was answered by a man who knocked her unconscious. She never saw the boyfriend again and was forced into prostitution in a brothel until some weeks later when she was drugged and brought into the UK in a car with one other young woman or girl. She had been held in a brothel in a flat in London for about eight months, where she was given nothing more than one burger a day to eat. She saw her opportunity to escape when her captor got caught up in an argument and was momentarily distracted. Isabel got out of the flat and out of the building, but knew that if she ran her captor would soon catch her. She made an astute decision to climb into the dustbin and covered herself with rubbish in case it was searched. She heard the commotion as her captors tried to find her but stayed still and waited. Eventually, after what she thinks may have been hours, she climbed out. Night had fallen and she had no idea where in the world she was but walked until she came to a train station. There was a woman there who, by chance, was Albanian, and who took Isabel to the police station where she was questioned but did not report that she had been in a brothel. When her case was heard in an immigration court about a year later, the UK Border Agency referred to her initial report as "a web of lies."

In those hours after she had escaped she did not know whom to trust. Women who have been trafficked are in grave danger of being re-trafficked. Street Talk has worked with some women who escaped from traffickers, then were re-trafficked. Traffickers deter women from trying to escape with threats, sometimes taking photographs of family in their own country and threatening that they will be killed should the woman try to get away. It seems reasonable for Isabel and others to be cautious what they say to whom, in those first hours. It is an abuse of the trafficked women's human rights to be forced to make a statement at a time when they feel acutely unsafe, which will be used in court.

Art Therapy

Art therapy was introduced as an experiment initially in the hostel for women who had escaped from traffickers, offering both group work and individual work. It was very successful especially for women who had little spoken English, giving them a way to express what they were living through. We now provide art therapy at the hostels and day centres for the street working women. Below some of the practitioners write about their work.

Catriona Alderton

Art has been used as a non-verbal method of communication for thousands of years. The creative arts are becoming more widely recognised as an effective way to maintain and improve mental health and well-being, build resilience and ease medical conditions. They are also a gentle method of dealing with personal trauma.

While art therapy can involve talking, it is not primarily a talking therapy. Working creatively with different media can connect directly with emotions and the subconscious. Seemingly random colours and shapes can coalesce into images representative of unresolved issues, or destructive patterns and behaviours which can then be worked through. It is a very gentle, but effective, form of therapy. In my experience, many people who have suffered are unwilling or unable to talk about their issues. Unresolved issues may then be suppressed and can lead to mental health problems or self-harming, or can sometimes be expressed as lashing out (aggression, anger). Working therapeutically with art enables the client to connect creatively with their subconscious and then work with (and through) the resulting images, making them 'safe', or transforming them.

Art therapy is also effective in a well-being context, for building resilience, assisting with emotional development and issues, helping improve social and team interactions, and reducing stress and anxiety.

Hannah

Hannah, aged fifty-seven, has struggled for decades with PTSD caused by repeated abuse issues which date from childhood. Other therapies hadn't helped and over time she'd developed coping strategies to survive. She self-harmed regularly (alcohol, drugs, cutting, bleach).

In one forty-five minute session she worked through a memory of an event which was repeated regularly, which involved being multiply abused, often in the same location. She worked spontaneously, dividing the paper in half with a vertical line. The left side developed a sketch of a female head; she had no idea what this represented. On the right, the words 'BLACK' and 'HOUSE' were written across each other to form an 'x' shape. She didn't know what the 'black house' signified initially, but said the words were often on her mind. Realisation dawned when she stopped and we observed the image together. She became distressed and reverted to childlike behaviour as she slipped into a flashback attack. Focussing on her breathing calmed her and averted the attack, and she was then asked how she wanted to make the image 'safe'. She quickly transformed it into a 'green' house by drawing over the black with green, adding flowers, door, windows and a smoking chimney. She reflected that the black lettering was still visible underneath the green. We discussed this, and she decided that in fact this was ok, as these past events could not be erased. On further reflection she announced that the face on the left was her younger self. She continued the work, becoming more confident, resorting less to self- harm, and began to develop a positive self-image.

Maria Xrisoula

I am sitting in the living room area of the hostel with T. She is obviously emotionally distressed. A difficult event has taken place in her private life and she reflects on her inability to say 'no' to people, even when she knows what the result will be. She accounts for similar events and how this 'always happens'.

She points at an art installation on the wall: decorated masks with glitter on a black canvas. One is gold, one is red and one is silver. The masks are positioned in an ascending order on the canvas. Underneath every mask there is one word respectively: Me, Myself and I.

'I made this as a symbol for that relationship with that previous lady [previous Street Talk art therapist]. I don't remember her name. I am in the middle now. In the red one. When I made it I was in the first. Next time this happens I will have to be on the third and then I will be able to say no.'

I was not present when that piece of artwork was done. T has been living in the house for six months and I have been working with her for three. The previous months she worked with my predecessor. T at the time did not verbally express the meaning behind her art. One can say that she might not have been ready at that particular time to reflect on it. Its presence in the living room on the other hand allowed for a sense of continuity in her process along with an objective point of reference, employed when she felt ready to reflect on the patterns of her behaviour and how they can be improved.

Winnicott says, 'the task of reality-acceptance is never completed, no human being is free from the strain of inner and outer reality, relief from this strain is provided by an intermediate area of experience which is not challenged.' (Winnicott 1971: p18).

Art therapy and the employment of creative tools, whether these take the form of poetry, painting, dancing, or sculpting, can provide that intermediate and unchallenged area of experience where things from our inner reality can slowly find a form of expression in the outer world, protected from interpretations, judgement or consequences. Instead whatever is created can hang on the wall or decorate the table or even be thrown in the bin. The one who creates the work can decide what will happen to it.

When working with addicts one has to acknowledge that the use of substances might serve as a solution to much more complex psychological issues. Consequently, addressing those underlying issues can become the solution to the addiction itself. Art therapy, due to its lack of necessity for words, can allow those issues to come to the room and be expressed and processed in ways that are more suitable for the users.

Winnicott says that it is only in being creative that the individual discovers the self (1971: p73). Similarly through art one can gain a sense of integrity. Our inner realities can be contradictive but within the safe space of a canvas opportunities can arise for reconciliation and integration.

Group Work

Street Talk had the opportunity to set up a therapy group for women at one of the day centres. In the usual spirit of experimentation, an open group, with weekly sessions of one hour, was offered to the women. In parallel with the individual therapy, it took years for the women to start to use the group. We staggered on over the first two years, when there were weeks when no women came or one woman came, or two women which does not constitute a group. It took about two years for the women who used the day centre to get the hang of what a group had to offer, but once women began to use the group it became a surprisingly successful intervention. We are extremely grateful to the partner charity who allowed us to persevere, trying to get the group going, allowing us the time it needed. There was a cohort of about fifteen women who committed to regular participation in the group. An average of six women attended each week with a group therapist and an assistant present. The success lay in the way in which the women seemed to find it easier to address difficult topics in the group than they did in individual therapy. It was interesting that some of the women who took part in the group were also in individual therapy with Street Talk but were able to speak about experiences in the group which they had not spoken about with their therapist. Women listened to one another attentively, respectfully and without judgement. Over four years there was only one occasion when a woman spoke disrespectfully to another.

It was interesting and surprising that women were able to use the group to discuss subjects which usually remain taboo, not only in informal conversation but also within the context of individual therapy. Over the four years that the group ran with good attendance, clear themes emerged. Those themes were:

Removal of children

Women particularly wanted to talk about the details of the moment of the removal. They wanted to talk about how it happened, where it happened, who was there, how they said goodbye to their child, how it felt at that moment, how it felt afterwards, how it feels now.

Separation from children

Women spoke about the pain of separation from children who were removed and who have been adopted, fostered or who are in a children's unit. The discussions focussed on the common feeling women had of having failed or abandoned their children. Women also spoke of their grief, the constant heartache and longing for their children, as well as their constant fears for their well-being. A common theme was the fear that those caring for their children might abuse them, that the children might be suffering. Women collectively suffered from a sense of powerlessness to protect their children. Women spoke about birthdays, the anniversary of when children were removed or when they saw them for the last time and about the fact that the year is punctuated by painful anniversaries. There was discussion of their contact with children who had been removed. A common theme was guilt at not taking up contact visits to their children. Unanimously women described these visits as unbearably painful. Many shared that they did not attend contact because they were not sure they could survive the grief; this included the very last contact with a child who had been placed for adoption. Women spoke about how it was unbearable to go to a visit at a children's centre to say goodbye to their child knowing that they would not see them again.

Overdose

Some women use substances in groups and many have had the grim experience of witnessing accidental overdoses, sometimes leading to death. Women spoke about the events which led up to such incidents in some detail, with a focus on whether an ambulance was called or not, who tried to help, who did nothing. Women frequently expressed intense guilt when they had not called for help or had not tried to resuscitate the person who died. They discussed their feelings towards the person who died, memories of that person and the confusing feelings of complicity and powerlessness. They discussed the consequences and whether anybody was arrested or charged. One woman spoke in the group about making a conscious choice not to try to resuscitate her partner when he accidentally overdosed, because in that moment she saw his death as her chance to free herself from his abuse and violence. Another told the group that she had allowed someone who had been present to be mistakenly arrested and charged for supplying, in the wake of an overdose, when in fact her boyfriend had been the supplier.

Arrest

Women reported the events surrounding their experiences of being arrested, being brutally treated, humiliated, beaten or verbally abused, their powerlessness and anger and their relationship with the authorities.

Violence

Street prostitution is characterised by violence. Punters are violent to the women, the drug dealers use violence to punish women and domestic violence and extreme bullying is common in their relationships. Women used the group to talk about their own violent behaviour to others, sometimes in self-defence, although not always, and explored their complex ambivalent feelings associated with that.

Bereavement

Women used the group to talk about their feelings about the deaths of family members, partners, children and other women. One third of the women had at least one child who had died, whilst more than half had lost a partner. The women are always deeply disturbed by the death of one of their own community, which leaves them feeling acutely vulnerable. Most of the premature deaths of the women are from chronic ill health combined with poor care and neglect.

Mental illness

Women spoke about how it feels to have a psychosis or a mania, about being put under section, the detailed events of exactly what happened and how that had felt. They discussed diagnoses and symptoms and there was a sense that women used the group to explore their own mental health history without stigma and without the difficulties encountered in a clinical context.

Clare and May

Clare had lived with bipolar disorder for twenty years. She had dual diagnosis and, despite being under the care of a mental health team, she had been arrested by the police for actions she carried out when she was psychotic: behaviour which was involuntary. She served a year on remand, in solitary confinement for some of that time, without treatment for her illness. She described to the group the terror of living through a psychosis, alone in a prison cell with no human contact. She also talked about the beatings she had from other prisoners when she was out of her cell, provoked by her psychotic behaviour, explaining that her broken nose which had not set straight was the result of a beating in prison.

Clare's generosity in sharing her experience of living with the illness and describing the symptoms enabled four other members of the group to identify with her experiences and symptoms. They were motivated to seek help, culminating in a diagnosis and treatment for the disease. None of the women had been diagnosed or treated previously. One of the group, May, was a grandmother in her sixties whose son had been removed from her care over fifty years ago. Her son had made attempts to contact her, but her shame had prevented her from responding. After hearing Clare describe the symptoms of bipolar, May suspected that she had been living with undiagnosed and untreated bipolar for as long as she could remember. May requested a mental health assessment, which resulted in a diagnosis of bipolar and treatment. She revisited the removal of her son, making sense of it in the context of her mental illness. She felt less shame and saw herself as someone who had been unable to cope with parenting because she had a chronic illness, rather than as someone who had abandoned her child. She made the decision to meet her son, as well as meeting her grandchildren for the first time. "I bloody found out I had been living with an illness all these years. Why did it take Clare to diagnose it? I have seen that many doctors all my life. She saw it straightaway and she's definitely not a doctor."

The group became a safe place for women to talk about extremely difficult topics and to work through old grief, perhaps because the shared experience made it possible to take more risks. Women were unfailingly supportive of one another; there was never any judgement and there was always at least one other member of the group who had shared something of the experience discussed. The therapists and assistant intervened minimally, creating a safe place where women set their own agenda and where they responded to one another's contributions. The therapists' roles were to open and close the group with a summing up of the feelings and themes which had been expressed over the course of the session. Apart from individual outcomes for the group members, the overwhelming outcome was that this experiment demonstrated that women with complex needs can engage creatively in therapeutic group work.

"Peers with similar experiences provide empathy, a living reminder of the possibility of change, relevant advice and reassurance that one is 'not alone'."

(Rethink, 2009; Deegan, 1988)

Outreach Legal Work

There is a lawyer who works *pro bono* for Street Talk. He meets with women to advise them on benefit, housing, family and criminal matters. It is a vital service, making bespoke legal advice accessible. There are women who have been on the run from legal matters for years, who have not had the capacity to access the appropriate legal advice, living in the shadows for fear that there is a warrant out for their arrest. In many cases the lawyer has been able to resolve legal complications quickly once he has interviewed a woman and understood the situation, which can make an enormous difference to a woman's mental health. The difficulty many women have in attending appointments has been referred to; it makes an enormous difference to have a lawyer who is willing to meet women in a place where they feel comfortable, at a time which works for them. There have been many cases where women have been unaware of their legal rights and in some cases the Street Talk lawyer has been able to advise them of their rights and obtain justice on their behalf. One woman came to Street Talk desperate that social services had reduced her visits to her child in foster care from weekly to monthly. She discovered through discussing her case with our lawyer that she had a legal right to take social services to court to prove her parenting capacity. The outcome was that the court awarded her full parental responsibility and her child came home to live with her permanently.

Campaigns

Street Talk has not had the capacity to run campaigns, but has lent its small weight to campaigns run by other organisations. Most recently these have included the campaign headed by Lord Dubbs to encourage the government to permit unaccompanied migrant children into the UK. The women Street Talk works with became vulnerable in childhood and their lives might have been saved if they had been taken care of when they were children. Street Talk has supported the campaign led by NIA to change the law regarding the criminal records of women convicted for offences relating to prostitution. They are currently listed as sex offenders.

Evaluation

The aim of the work is to enable women to encounter their own humanity. What we have learned is that if a woman can feel human again the hard outcomes ensue. It is hard to identify and account for the moment when a woman feels worth something; it may come at a time when a woman is not in contact with the therapist, in a moment of reflection, or it may be a gradual dawning, over years. However, it is that shift in self-perception which is the crucial change which needs to take place in order for the more tangible, more easily measured, progress to occur. Conversely, no matter how much help with practical issues is offered, help with addiction, housing, benefits and so forth, they will add up to nothing and a woman will relapse sooner or later if she does not have a sense of her entitlement to live safely and with dignity. The horse which comes before the cart is the woman's sense of self-worth.

Whilst the hard outcomes – a success in court, abstinence from substance use, contact with family, getting off the street – are important, there is a danger that in measuring the work by counting the hard outcomes one misses the point. Even when women achieve no hard outcomes, the work to enable a woman to experience her own humanity and to feel worth something, remains worthwhile. Prescriptive outcome measures can work as a subtly oppressive force against women, placing value on them when they achieve a particular outcome but refusing to notice them when they do not achieve that outcome.

Payment by results depends on a pre-determined definition of a "result" which usually precludes the client's lived experience and unique situation. Some funders, who are not necessarily experts in the sector, set hoops which the client is expected to jump through. More informed funders, for example Comic Relief and Trust For London, both of whom have funded Street Talk, work together with us to identify appropriate targets. Services are increasingly expected to meet unrealistic targets turning the client into little more than a performing monkey. It is important to work with the women to evaluate the service. They know, better than anyone else can ever know, whether a service is working.

Nina

Nina was seeing the Street Talk counsellor over a period of several months. Over that time she never reduced her using, never exited prostitution, never moved out of the hostel into a place of her own, never got even close to working out what her goals might be, let alone achieving any of them, before her life came to a premature end. One might claim that she made no progress, that the work had been a waste of resources. However, Nina had known nothing but cruelty, violence and exploitation. If, at some point in the work with Street Talk, she got even the most transient sense of a different kind of human relationship, where she was something other than currency, then that work needs no other justification. If Nina encountered her own humanity, even for one moment, before her life ended this was a good piece of work. It has been worth setting Street Talk up if only for that woman.

It is important to evaluate the work. The challenge is to communicate the value of intangible outcomes which can't be quantified to stakeholders. Street Talk returned a grant to funders who wanted to set outcomes which were unrealistic. When outcome measures fail to capture the value of work, that can diminish the work. It is an issue across the sector, not one which is exclusive to Street Talk. There is a need to measure work creatively. Reductionist, tick the box exercises cannot reflect the complexity of this work.

Supporting Women through Family Court Proceedings

The removal of children is one of the most important aspects of the lives of the women who come to Street Talk. There are occasions when a woman who is working with Street Talk is not well enough or does not have the capacity to take care of her child. Street Talk works in co-operation with social services, reporting concerns for a child when those occur.

Street Talk supports women around the removal of children in a number of different ways. There are women who become pregnant at a time when they are extremely vulnerable but who find their motivation to recover in the desire to become a good mother. Street Talk supports women to fight for the right to a parenting assessment. It is usually a fight for women in street based prostitution; that word is used advisedly. The ethos of Street Talk is that anyone can recover and on that basis Street Talk will support every woman's right to a parenting assessment. Over the years there have been women who have been allowed a parenting assessment but who have been assessed as unfit to parent their own child. In those cases, the work of Street Talk is to provide support at a time when a woman is most in need and most vulnerable.

There have been a number of cases where social services have wanted the child to be placed for adoption without a parenting assessment. Some of the women we have worked with have fought against that in court, been awarded the right to a parenting assessment, have succeeded and have gone on to provide a loving home. Over the last thirteen years Street Talk has worked closely with fourteen women who fought against having their children adopted. All women eventually were awarded full parental responsibility through the courts following the due process of assessment which was carried out over several years. The various judges in the family court in those cases have always thanked Street Talk for their work with the women when social services had not wanted to give them a chance. Out of those fourteen families, all but one continue to do really well, all of their children are thriving and they are making excellent mothers. One woman, referred to in the case history above with the given name Laura, did not manage and her child was removed at a later date. That is extremely sad for Laura's child, as it is for Laura. Out of fourteen families there are thirteen who are together and doing well, where the cycle of growing up in the state care system has been broken.

One small way in which Street Talk supports women who have not been reunited with their children is to archive a letter from the mother to the children. Women take comfort at the point of removal, or in later years, knowing that if their children should come searching for them when they become adults, there may be a letter to give the child, written by their mother. The letters all say the same thing, that their mother wanted to keep them, tried her best to keep them and that they love them. It may be, in the future, that some of those children may be equally comforted by those letters, should they make contact. There is particular poignancy to that work because some of those women will not live long enough to meet their children when they grow up and the women are well aware of that.

There is a failure in the system to represent the mother's voice in the records when children are removed. Adults trying to find out why they were adopted are usually told that there was neglect, abuse, heroin addiction and so forth. The words "The mother loved heroin more than she loved her child" occur in many social service reports. Street Talk has never met a woman who loved heroin more than she loved her child. There is addiction and chaos and sometimes neglect but those are only part of the picture: consequences, not causes. The mother is a victim of her past and is paying the price for that, but loves her children as much as any mother. Most of the women put up the fight of their life to be able to have a parenting assessment and a chance of keeping their child, but no record is kept of that. One woman had her baby removed several days after the birth, then stood outside the hospital, day and night through two weeks in January, just fixing her gaze on the window of the room she thought he was in, although the building was several storeys high and there was no chance of getting a glimpse of the baby. She was only persuaded to leave when she learned that he had been taken from the hospital to foster carers. Street Talk has archived an account of that so that if in the future he researches his mother he will know that she loved him.

Volunteer Programme for Women

When women begin to feel their self-worth, without exception they want to do something to help other women. Harnessing one's own suffering to work to prevent suffering in others seems intrinsic to recovery.

> *"Identity is strongly tied to meaningful roles in life, which validate new positive identities, making people feel part of the 'mainstream' and giving self-worth. Longitudinal data shows a strong association between higher life quality and engagement in meaningful activity."*
> (Best and Lubman, 2012)

The problem is that opportunities for women to volunteer are difficult to find. Women who have been convicted for soliciting are listed as sex offenders and do not want to have to disclose that, which prevents them from taking volunteering opportunities. In response Street Talk has a volunteering programme which offers women who have made progress, who are abstinent and well enough, to act as mentors or to help in other ways according to their interests. Ideally, women would find another organisation to volunteer with because that might give them more of a sense of achievement, of having grown up and left home, but the volunteer programme with Street Talk offers a stepping stone.

Referral Network

Referring women to other agencies for specialist professional help or other opportunities is an important aspect of the work. The point has already been made that women make progress when they engage with multiple organisations. Referrals to addiction, health and specialist advice services are the most common. Street Talk has a close link with the HERA programme, which offers excellent educational opportunities and a training in enterprise for vulnerable women, as well as with other organisations which offer volunteering or educational opportunities.

Remaining Small

Street Talk intends to remain a small charity where it will be possible to maintain the highest possible professional standards and quality of work whilst taking care of those undertaking this challenging work. There is a sea of need and it is hoped that, rather than Street Talk trying to expand to meet that need, other groups might replicate something of the model. There is pressure from stakeholders to expand but the integrity of the work is why we do this, and the only way to ensure that is to remain a small organisation. Along the way, there have been stakeholders who have encouraged a business model and in particular rapid expansion. The quality of the work depends on those managing the services having a close relationship with the therapists. That would not be possible if the organisation became bigger. It is hoped that others working in the sector might share the learning and in that way this therapeutic model might reach more vulnerable women.

Challenges

Keeping Staff Safe

Therapists are at risk of vicarious trauma, working with clients who have not only lived through trauma in their past but who are encountering violence on the street on a day to day basis. A further challenge for therapists engaging with women caught up in a repeating cycle of trauma, situated at the intersection of multiple social injustices, is that the therapist can feel as powerless as the woman. The work is to bear witness, to accompany and, where possible, to engage in an on-going creative therapeutic process. There are occasions when that feels too little. Part of the challenge of the work is to value the little that one can do. I think of the day when I was in court with Sarah who was hoping to get her baby back from care, following a positive parenting assessment. The judge addressed her directly, asking, "What plans do you have in place to take the baby home?" Sarah jumped out of her seat for joy and shouted, "I am taking the baby home!" She then turned to me and said, "I haven't brought the carrycot." The judge interrupted, "Exactly! As I thought. No plans in place. She couldn't possibly cope."

She went on to place the child on a care order, before addressing Sarah's social worker to ask, "Is she pregnant again? When is her next period due?" Sarah ran from the court and my experience in that moment was one of utter powerlessness before the inhumanity.

The following practices are in place to protect therapists from vicarious trauma as far as possible:

- Case load limited to six clients per therapist.
- High ratio of supervision to therapy.
- Team meetings where cases can be discussed and team members can support one another.
- Relevant specialist training made available.
- Sabbaticals for therapists permitted.
- An ethos where it is safe to say if the work has become disturbing and a therapist needs to do less, take some time off or stop.

Finding People who can do the Work

This is not work which suits everybody. The challenges are many and the work requires exceptional patience, resilience, adaptability and humility. Therapists need to feel confident in their practice, as well as being well trained and well qualified. They need to come to this work with some experience of working with people with complex needs. The four stage model outlined above differs from the model of object relations work which therapists were taught when they trained and have practised over many years in other contexts, and not every therapist would want to practise differently.

The Need for Resilience

Street Talk therapists are exposed to abuse; we have all been sworn at many times. Our understanding is that when a woman tells us to "fuck off!" it is because they are in what I have come to refer to as "the fuck off place". It is a cry of pain or despair, from a feeling of worthlessness. It is never personal and mostly, after they have sworn at one of the therapists, women will find them and will apologise. It isn't easy to be abused but it is easier to work with when you understand the context and that it is a projection.

The second phase of the therapy, referred to as passive creative, demands therapists who are both tenacious and emotionally robust.

It is hard to turn up week after week for someone who may or may not be there, who might have drifted away without a word, whose whereabouts are a mystery, or who, if they are there, might tell you to go away. There have been occasions when therapists haven't known whether the client they are waiting for is alive or dead.

Partnership Model

Working in partnership brings challenges at an organisational level. Providing a service to a hostel or day centre is not unlike being a guest in someone's house. Clients are always shared clients and there are times when the host charity makes a decision concerning a client which the Street Talk therapist would not have made, but has to accept because there is a responsibility to work well alongside the partner organisation. A strong service level agreement from the outset is essential. One of the benefits of the partnership model is that women seem to be able to trust an external therapist more readily.

Funding

It does not need pointing out that funding work where the focus is on the intangible outcome of encountering one's own humanity is challenging. It is known that women's charities, addiction, mental health, homelessness and domestic violence are not popular causes; throw prostitution into the mix and that adds a whole new level of difficulty. The challenge in fundraising for women in prostitution lies in the semantics: it is not realistic to expect funders to engage in a dialogue about the different activities referred to by that term.

Organisations are influenced by who they choose to take funding from. To preserve the integrity of the work one has to be careful that funders are sympathetic to the Street Talk model and that they want to fund work which is not driven by hard outcomes. Street Talk is committed to work which remains client-led, where the only outcomes which matter are those which have meaning to the client.

Conclusion

In her foreword, Jan Birtle referred to my struggle to write about all that we have learned from the women. Street Talk has worked with hundreds of women, each of whom has a story which everyone should hear and each of which exposes specific injustice and systemic failures in the provision of care for vulnerable people. My struggle has been to decide what to leave out. It has been a privilege to work with the women, and the responsibility to honour their courage and dignity weighs heavily. I have left out the most brutal and sickening details of the abuse which women suffered in their childhood and in some cases in their day to day lives because it is too hard to write about and would be too hard to read. I do acknowledge that my reticence reflects the way in which the women and other professionals are silenced by the unspeakable nature of the women's experiences.

The most important thing I have learned is that anyone can engage in therapy and that everyone has the potential to recover. Some of those women who seemed the least likely to engage and the most broken when they came to Street Talk have made a full recovery. It is never time to give up on someone.

> " ... many can and do, find agency, hope, and meaning via an undoubtedly long and difficult journey."
>
> (Farrall et al, 2014)

> "A meaningful, dignified and gratifying life is very possible including where severe mental illness does not ever disappear for good."
>
> (Davidson and Roe, 2007)

The other thing I have learned is that people who are made vulnerable by childhood trauma are brutalised and re-traumatised by the state in adulthood, and we all have a collective responsibility in that. Whilst this work has set out to show that, with small adaptations, therapy can become accessible to women who have been excluded from care, therapy should not be used to mask socio-economic oppression. Disadvantage, exclusion and prejudice remain present, no matter how much progress women make in their therapy. It is important not to conflate social oppression with individual trauma, neurosis or mental illness. A woman can recover in terms of her trauma and self-esteem, but still encounter insurmountable social injustice and economic inequality which can overshadow and dismantle her recovery. There are some women's prisons which now give sleeping bags to women on their release because it is known they have nowhere to go but the most dangerous place of all: the street.

> *"Living in a precarious space such as a squat or a violent and deprived neighbourhood is a barrier to recovery, associated with exploitation, vulnerability and danger."*
>
> (Leverentz, 2014)

The deepening injustices in our society are creating greater and more widespread suffering among the most vulnerable. Rough sleeping is up 134% since 2000. Therapy has its place in enabling vulnerable women to live in safety and with dignity, but a fairer, more even society would do more. Perhaps the response offered by therapy to women who are at the sharp end of social injustice is to work to enable them to identify the abuse which accompanies social injustice, just as therapy enables women to recognise abuse in their personal life. I am going to give the last word to one of our women. Fleur was trafficked from Vietnam at the age of fourteen.

At the end of our work together she made a card for me. Inside she had written, "You looked at me."

Appendix:
Bibliography

All Party Parliamentary Group on Complex Needs and Dual Diagnosis 2011 available at www.turning-point. co.uk/media/appg response to the NHS future forum – key issues facing excluded groups 2011.pdf

Ajayi, S. et al. 2009. *Getting back into the world: Reflections on lived experiences of recovery.* London: Rethink Recovery Series Vol 2

Anderson, R. (ed.) 1991. *Clinical Lectures on Klein and Bion.* New Library of Psychoanalysis, Routledge

Anderson, S. Dickie, E. Parker, C. 2013. *Street Talk: An Evaluation of a counselling service for women involved in street based prostitution and victims of trafficking.* Revolving Doors

Anderson, S. 2016. The value of 'bearing witness' to desistence. *Probation Journal*

Aranson, J. 1981. *The Work of Hanna Segal: A Kleinian approach to clinical practice.* London: Free Associations Books, 1986

Benyon, R. 2010. What health problems do homeless street sex workers face and what can be done to improve their situation? Available at www.healthy-inclusion.org.uk/wpcontent/uploads/downloads/2010

Best, D. W. and Lubman, D. I. 2012. The recovery paradigm: A Model of hope and change for alcohol and drug addiction. *Australian family physician*, 41

Bion, W. R. 1932. *Learning from experience*. Heinemann. Reprinted by Karnac Books, 1989

Bion, W. R. 1963. *Elements of psychoanalysis*. Heinemann. Reprinted by Karnac Books, 1989

Bion, W. R. 1970. *Attention and interpretation*. Tavistock. Reprinted by Karnac Books, 1988

Bowlby, J. 1965. *Child care and the growth of love*. Penguin

Bowlby, J. 1990. *A Secure base*. Basic Books

Bowlby, J. 1998. *Attachment and loss trilogy*. Penguin

Bramley, G. and Fitzpatrick, S. with Edwards J. Ford, D. Johnsen, S. Sosenko F. and Watkins D. 2015. *Hard edges: mapping severe and multiple disadvantage across England*. London: Lankelly Chase

Branovic, B. and Bjelajac, Z. 2012. Traumatic experiences, psychophysical consequences and needs of human trafficking victims. *Vojnosaniteski Pregled*, 69(1)

Briere, J. and Scott, C. 2006. *Principles of trauma therapy: A Guide to symptoms, evaluation, and treatment*. London: Sage

Brison, S.J. 1999. Trauma narratives and the remaking of the self. In: Bal, M. Spitzer, L. Crewe, J.V. (eds.), *Acts of memory: Cultural recall in the present*. Hanover, NH: University Press of New England

Carver, R. 1994. *A New path to the waterfall*. Atlantic Monthly Press

Casement, P. 1985. *Learning from the patient*. London: Routledge

Casement, P. 1986. Countertransference and interpretation. *Contemporary Psychoanalysis*, Vol. 22: No 4

Casement, P. 1990. *Further learning from the patient*. London: Routledge

Casement, P. 2002. *Learning from our mistakes: Beyond dogma in psychoanalysis and psychotherapy*. London: Routledge

Casement, P. 2011. Imprisoned minds. *American Imago*, 287–295

Casement, P. 2017. Ways of working: A Synopsis of contributions to psychoanalytic technique. *BPAS bulletin* (October 2017) and *International Journal of Psychoanalysis* 6

Corston, J. 2007. Corston report, a report by Baroness Jean Corston: A Review of women with particular vulnerabilities in the criminal justice system

Davidson, L., and Roe, D. 2007. Recovery from versus recovery in serious mental illness: One strategy for lessening confusion plaguing recovery. *Journal of Mental Health*, 16

Deegan, P. E. 1988. Recovery: The Lived experience of rehabilitation. *Psychosocial Rehabilitation Journal*, 11

Erikson, E. F. 1994. *Identity*. New York: Norton

Erikson, E. F. 1998. *The Life cycle completed*. New York: Norton

Fairbairn, W. R. D. 1952. *An Object-Relations Theory of the Personality*. New York: Basic Books.

Farrall, S. 2005. On the existential aspects of desistance from crime. *Symbolic Interaction*, Vol. 28, Issue 3

Farrall, S. Calverley, A. 2006. *Understanding desistance from crime: Emerging theoretical directions in rehabilitation and resettlement*. Maidenhead: Open University Press

Farrall, S. Hunter, B. Sharpe, G. and Calverley, A. 2014. *Criminal careers in transition: The Social context of desistance from crime*. Oxford: Oxford University Press

Gately, E. 1990. *I hear a seed growing*. Chicago: Source Books

Gomez, L. 1997. *An Introduction to object relations theory*. London: Free Association Press

Harris, J. and McElrath, K. 2012. Methadone as social control: Institutionalized stigma and the prospect of recovery. *Qualitative Health Research*, Vol. 22

Harvey, H. Brown, L. and Young, L. 2017. *"I'm no criminal."* London NIA

Henwood, B. F. Padgett, D. K. Smith, B. T. and Tiderington, E. 2012. Substance abuse recovery after experiencing homelessness and mental illness: Case studies of change over time. *Journal of dual diagnosis*, 8

Herman, J. 1997. *Trauma and recovery*. New York: Basic Books

Holmes, C. 2005. *The Paradox of countertransference*. Palgrave McMillan

Jacobson, N. and Greenley, D. 2001. What is recovery? A conceptual model and explication. *Psychiatric services*, Vol. 52

Kalathil, J. 2011. *Recovery and resilience: African, African-Caribbean and South Asian women's narratives of recovering from mental distress*. London: Mental Health Foundation

Klein, M. 1932. *The psychoanalysis of children*

Klein, M. Envy and Gratitude and other works. Melanie Klein Trust, 1946–1963

Klein, M. 1975. Love, guilt and reparation and other works 19211945 (*The Writings of Melanie Klein, Vol. 1*). Hogarth Press

Klein, M. Heimann, P. Isaacs, S. and Rivière J. 1952. *Developments in psychoanalysis*.

Klein, M. and Rivière, J. Love, hate, and reparation. (*Psychoanalytical Epitomes No. 2*) 1937, reprinted in 1953

Leverentz, A.M. 2014. *The ex-prisoner's dilemma: how women negotiate competing narratives of re-entry and desistance*. New Brunswick, New Jersey: Rutgers University Press

Lopez-Corvo, R. 2006. *Wild thoughts searching for a thinker: a clinical application of W.R. Bion's theories*. Karnac Books

Maruna, S. 2001. *Making good: how ex-convicts reform and rebuild their lives*. London: American Psychological Association

Menzies Lyth, I. 1988. *Containing anxiety in institutions: selected essays*. London: Free Association Books

O'Shaughessy, E. 1993. Words and working through. *International Journal of Psycho-Analysis* 64

Perlesz, A. 1999. Complex responses to trauma: challenges in bearing witness. *Australian and New Zealand Journal of Family Therapy*, vol. 20

Petot, J. 1991. *Melanie Klein: The Ego and the good object 1932–1960*. Translated by C. Trollope. Connecticut: International Universities Press

Robertson, J. and Robertson, J. 1971. Young children in brief separation: a fresh look. *Psychoanalytic Study of the Child*, vol. 26

Rosenfeld, H. A. 1964. *Psychotic States*. London: Hogarth Press

Spillius, E. and O'Shaughessy, E. (eds.) 2011. *Projective identification: the fate of a concept.* Routledge.

Terry, L. 2015. *A Good life: exploring what matters to people facing multiple and complex needs*. London: Revolving Doors

Wagner, M. The Work of James and Joyce Robertson. Available at www.childdevelopmentmedia.com/articles/classic-treasures-thework-of-james-and-joyce-robertson

Winnicott, D. W. 1971. *Playing and reality*. Tavistock, London and New York

Winnicott, D.W. 1986. *Holding and interpretation: fragment of an analysis*. Karnac Books

Winnicott, D.W. 1990. *The Maturational processes and the facilitating environment: studies in the theory of emotional development*. London: Karnac Books

Winnicott, D.W. 2010. *Psycho-analytic explorations*. London: Karnac Books

Yalom, I. and Leszcz, M. 2005. *The Theory and practice of group psychotherapy*. New York: Basic Books